T0112694

The Poverty of Growth

The Poverty of Growth

Olivier De Schutter

Foreword by Kate Raworth

First published 2024 by Pluto Press
New Wing, Somerset House, Strand, London WC2R 1LA
and Pluto Press, Inc.
1930 Village Center Circle, 3-834, Las Vegas, NV 89134

www.plutobooks.com

British Library Cataloguing in Publication Data
A catalogue record for this book is available from the British Library

ISBN 978 0 7453 5023 3 Paperback
ISBN 978 0 7453 5025 7 PDF
ISBN 978 0 7453 5024 0 EPUB

This book is printed on paper suitable for recycling and made from fully
managed and sustained forest sources. Logging, pulping and manufacturing
processes are expected to conform to the environmental standards of the
country of origin.

Typeset by Stanford DTP Services, Northampton, England

Simultaneously printed in the United Kingdom and United States of America

Contents

Foreword by Kate Raworth   vii

Preface   xi

Abbreviations   xix

Introduction   1

1   What is Poverty?   5

2   Is Economic Growth the Solution?   14

3   The Strange Persistence of the Ideology of Growth   53

4   The Post-growth Approach to Combating Poverty   61

Conclusion   95

Notes   97

Foreword

Kate Raworth

Here's a question for our times: how should we imagine the shape of progress?

In the twentieth century the answer may have seemed to be very clear. It was growth, measured in terms of national income, or gross domestic product (GDP). And that growth was to be endless, an ever-rising curve. No matter how rich a nation already was, its politicians and economists would consistently claim that the solutions to its problems depended on yet more growth.

As this book powerfully sets out, this last-century promise that economic growth will enable high-income countries to overcome their problems – whether problems of poverty or pollution – has not delivered. It is clearly time to reimagine the shape of progress and, with it, the policies that could bring about a twenty-first-century prosperity for a fractured humanity on a destabilized planet.

Stepping back, it's useful first to recognize the appeal of growth. It is, after all, a wonderful, healthy phase of life, which is why people the world over love to see children, gardens and trees grow. No wonder the Western mind so readily accepted it as the shape of economic progress too, and simultaneously adopted the very twentieth-century mantra that 'more is better', both personally and nationally.

Yet if we look to nature, it's clear that nothing in the living world succeeds by growing forever: anything that seeks to do so will, in the process, destroy itself or the system on which it depends. In nature things that succeed grow until they are grown up, at which point they mature, enabling them to thrive, sometimes for hundreds of years. As the Biomimicry pioneer Janine Benyus reminds us, a tree keeps on growing only up to the point that it is still able to send nutrients to the leaves at the outermost tips of its branches, at which point it stops. Its pursuit of growth is bounded by a greater goal of distributing and circulating the resources that nurture and sustain the health of its whole being.

Although we can appreciate the nuanced role, value and limits of growth in the living world, when it comes to the design of our economies, we have been acculturated to perceive growth as a constant aspiration and necessity. Thanks to the availability of cheap fossil-based energy in the twentieth century, the rapid and persistent economic growth that this enabled in industrialized countries soon came to be seen as normal and natural, indeed as essential. Its continuation over many decades led to the creation of institutional designs and policies – from credit creation to shareholder dividends to pension funds – that are structurally dependent on growth without end. In other words, we have inherited economies that need to grow, whether or not they make us thrive.

This requirement for endless growth has become so locked into economic theories, political narratives and public expectations that, over recent decades, governments have made clear the desperate and often destructive measures they are willing to go to into order to reboot growth when it becomes elusive. They deregulate – or rather re-regulate – finance in the hope of unleashing new productive investment, but often end up unleashing speculative bubbles, house price hikes and debt crises instead. They promise corporations that they will 'cut red tape' but end up dismantling legislation that was put in place to protect workers' rights, community residents and the living world. They privatize public services – from hospitals to railways – turning public wealth into private revenue streams that so often undermine the very services they claim to provide. They add the living world into the national accounts as 'ecosystem services' and 'natural capital', assigning it a value that looks dangerously like a price. And, despite committing to keep global heating 'well below 2°C', they open up new licensing for fossil fuel exploration, while failing to make the scale of transformational public investments needed for a renewable energy revolution. These policy choices are akin to throwing precious cargo off a plane that is running out of fuel, rather than admitting it is time to touch down and instead create post-growth economies that focus on delivering social and ecological health and integrity.

As Olivier De Schutter so compellingly argues here, the insistent pursuit of growth in high-income countries is not only preventing carbon emissions and material consumption from being reduced at the speed and scale that these times urgently demand. It is also failing to tackle poverty and endemic social inequalities – the very problems for which growth is so often offered as the remedy. Indeed the book's key contribution is its message that the pursuit of growth has become 'counter-productive' to the mission of tackling poverty. The policy tools that are so commonly used to stimulate growth – creating 'business-friendly' environments through privatization, commodification and trade liberalization – in fact have all too often widened inequalities and created the very social exclusion that growth was promised as a means to address.

Instead of pursuing endless growth it is time to pursue a thriving well-being for all people as part of a thriving living world, with policymaking that is designed to be in service to this goal. And this means putting human well-being and ecological integrity at the heart of our vision for economic success. Starting with the goal of human well-being within planetary boundaries results in a very different shape of progress: in the place of endless growth we find a dynamic balance, one that aims to meet the essential needs of every person while protecting the life-supporting systems of our planetary home. And since we are the inheritors of economies that need to grow, whether or not they make us thrive, a critical economic challenge in high-income countries is to create economies that enable us to thrive, whether or not they grow.

As this book argues, tackling and reversing inequalities needs to be at the heart of a new eco-social contract because doing so can deliver major impacts, both in terms of improving well-being – including self-expressed life satisfaction – and in terms of reducing nations' ecological footprints, due to the well-documented links between social inequalities and consumption impacts.

Tackling inequalities is also critical for reasons of political economy. One of the most damaging consequences of growth that exacerbates economic inequalities is the concentration of wealth and economic power in few hands. This can all too easily be converted into political power to influence elections and policymaking processes, to ensure that policies are retracted, enacted or recrafted to preserve the systemic advantages of the already wealthy. There is, in other words, a tacit market for political influence, and it is used to ensure that inequalities of wealth, power and voice are perpetuated.

When we turn away from growth as the goal we can focus directly on asking what it will take to deliver social and ecological well-being. And while many of the policies that this brings to the fore were, only a decade ago, considered too radical to be realistic, they are now gaining public interest, leading to animated discussion and serious policy consideration. This book makes an invaluable contribution to furthering the rationale and realism of exploring such policies, so that we can start to focus on creating economies that thrive in balance by meeting the needs of all people within the means of the living planet.

Kate Raworth
December 2023

Preface

As a means to fight against poverty and inequalities, economic growth has passed the peak of its usefulness: in rich countries, it has become counter-productive.

Understood as the increase of gross domestic product (GDP) – the total value of economic output within society – economic growth has long been seen as an indispensable tool to reduce poverty and inequalities. In what came to be known as the 'Bretton-Woods era', running roughly between the end of the Second World War and the economic crisis of 1973, the deal was simple: the value created by productivity gains was to be shared between shareholders, workers and the state, respectively, in the form of dividends on corporate income, wages and taxes.

This was the so-called 'Fordist compromise': economic growth was pursued by a mix of technological progress and the gradual removal of barriers to cross-country trade and investment, allowing the strengthening of the welfare state. Prosperity increased, and it was broadly spread. Between 1950 and 1973, GDP growth in industrialized countries averaged 3.72 per cent per year, leading to a doubling of the value of economic output. During this same period, the share of the public sector in these countries rose from 27 to 43 per cent of GDP, and social transfers rose from 7 to 15 per cent. In the United States, average annual growth per capita during this period was 3.91 per cent, and the share of the public sector in the GDP increased from 21.4 per cent to 31.1 per cent. In the United Kingdom, while GDP per capita growth was slightly less impressive (increasing annually by 2.4 per cent on average), the role of public services and social protection followed a similar pattern: the share of the public sector in the GDP increased from 34.2 per cent to 41.5 per cent.[1]

This came at a price, however. It led to what Earth scientists now call the 'Great Acceleration'.[2] These scientists highlight the relationship between changes in human production and consumption, measured by indicators such as GDP, direct foreign investment, energy consumption and telecommunications, to changes in the Earth's natural systems, including in particular climate and ocean acidification, and terrestrial biosphere degradation. Since 1973, we have been living beyond the biocapacity of the Earth: we consume more resources than are naturally replenished, and we dump into the environment more waste and pollution than the ecosystems can absorb.

Economic growth has thus led us to cross a number of planetary boundaries, or to dangerously approach them. It has eroded our natural capital. But it has also depleted our social and human capital, breaking down communities and exhausting working women and men.

In the name of stimulating growth, we have deregulated the labour market. New forms of sub-standard and atypical employment contracts have been introduced. A global precariat has emerged, subject to unpredictable working schedules and forced to accept wage levels below what is necessary to achieve a decent standard of living. They form what Guy Standing describes as a 'new dangerous class', sometimes referred to in the United States as the 'underclass'.[3] Work has been intensified in the search for increased productivity. Barriers to trade and investment were further lowered, making the position of the least qualified workers more fragile and weakening the bargaining position of unions in high-wage jurisdictions. Again in the name of growth, governments have sought to shape a 'business-friendly investment climate' – the code in these times for signalling that taxes and regulations on business would be reduced.

Thus, over the past forty years, the quest for economic growth has created exclusion and has led to a massive increase of inequalities.

This short book is based on the conviction that the fight against poverty and inequalities can be framed differently. Economic growth, understood as the increase of the output of economic activity measured in monetary terms, remains important in order to make progress in certain areas, such as housing, education or public transport, especially to raise living standards in low-income countries, which still need to invest massively in order to alleviate poverty by improving the provision of public services. Even in these countries however, GDP growth should not be fetishized: what matters is not whether that indicator increases, but whether the well-being of the population improves. *Selective* growth, thus understood, may be required to improve the fulfilment of basic needs through the provision of public services and social protection: as Kate Raworth eloquently argued, the challenge is to ensure the protection of a floor of social outcomes, while not exceeding the ceiling of planetary boundaries.[4]

In rich countries, however, we need something else: not economic growth intended to create wealth, with its damaging impacts on people and the environment we must then make up for, but a truly inclusive economy, designed to prevent poverty and inequalities. Poverty and inequalities should not be seen as an inevitable consequence of the progress of capitalism that we should tolerate before trying to remedy their impacts: they should be seen, instead, as a symptom of an economy that has become ill-suited to the aim of a shared and sustainable prosperity. We must now move from an extractive and predatory economy to a non-violent economy; from an economy that responds to the demand expressed by the superior purchasing power of the rich to one that caters to the basic needs of the poor; from an economy, finally, that excludes and ranks, to one that includes and values the contribution of each member of society. In order to achieve this, we first need to get rid of what Jason Hickel calls the ideology of growthism: at best, the belief that growth, as a measure of the total output of the economy, is a necessary precondition for addressing the societal challenges we face; and at worst, that it is a desirable goal in itself.[5] Twenty years ago, the ecological economist Clive Hamilton arrived at the conclusion that 'the more we examine the role of growth in modern society, the more our obsession with growth appears to be a fetish – that is, an inanimate object worshipped for its apparent magical powers'.[6] These words resonate today more powerfully even than they resonated then.

The current threats to the Earth systems leave us no choice: we must move swiftly towards transforming societies. This is both inevitable and urgent. The social and ecological transformation we need can be built on such a non-violent economy, provided we see this transformation as a lever to achieve social justice. I try to show in this book how we could move in this direction. In the choice of measures aiming to deliver the ecological transformation, we should prioritize measures that produce a 'triple dividend': measures that reduce our ecological footprint, but that at the same time create employment opportunities and ensure that the goods and services required for a decent life are affordable to low-income households. In the design of our tax and social policies, we can do more to reduce inequalities of income and wealth. This would reassure the members of the lower middle class who fear losing ground. It would also reduce the incentive to achieve social status through conspicuous forms of consumption. It would address, more generally, the status anxiety that largely explains the persistence of unsustainable lifestyles aimed chiefly at meeting real or imaginary social expectations. In the field of employment, finally, we could combine the idea of a 'job guarantee', ensuring that the state acts as employment of last resort, with a generalized reduction of working time and the democratization of work.

These instruments could go a long way towards reconciling public opinion, and particularly low-income households, with the ecological transformation: ensuring that such a transformation is seen as an opportunity rather than as a burden. Moving towards a low-carbon society that maintains and enhances biodiversity does not require that painful sacrifices should be imposed on the population. It is rather the opposite. It means investing in public transport, in the insulation of buildings, in agroecological food production, or in other measures that create jobs, favour access to goods and services at an affordable price, and stem environmental destruction. It means treating the ecological transformation as a springboard for social cohesion and for the reconstitution of social capital, this 'cement of society' that favours the emergence of collective action on the basis of trust, and thus allows for the replenishment and nurturing of the commons.[7] It means, finally, moving towards a society that is less work-centred, but that at the same time guarantees access to meaningful work for all of its members, in the organization of which they will be able to participate.

This change in direction requires individuals and societies that are truly autonomous, and therefore able to revise inherited understandings of 'happiness' and 'progress', and to lucidly reassess the trajectory they seek to pursue. This is why I emphasize the 'sufficiency norm' that should guide our behaviour, noting that the choice of such a norm is eminently the result of an exercise in self-determination, the very opposite of the tame complying with the injunction to consume that makes us, in Günther Anders' words, 'home workers' in the service of capitalist growth. This is also why I note that societies equipped to achieve the ecological and social transformation required should be further democratized, to avoid capture by the most powerful economic actors. These actors promise to deliver mass production to allow for mass consumption. They have a superior ability to achieve economies of scale and to control global networks of production. This is what explains their political influence: large corporations, operating transnationally, have become indispensable to our wasteful lifestyles, based on a permanent renewal of the things that surround us and to which we have become so deeply addicted.

Individuals and societies should escape the trap that has closed upon them. With his usual lucidity, Cornelius Castoriadis expressed his diagnosis of our late modernity as follows:

> There are no limits to the progress of our 'power' (and of our 'wealth'); or, to put things differently, whatever limits do exist are valued negatively and [seen as obstacles that] must be overcome.... The movement is towards more and more; more commodities, longer life expectancies, more scientific publications, more people with a doctorate – and 'more' is 'better'.... It is thus that we arrive at the present situation. Historical and social development consists in moving away from any defined state, in attaining a state which is defined by nothing except by the capacity to attain new states. The norm is that there is no norm. Historic and social development is an infinite deployment, a deployment without an end (in both meanings of the word 'end').[8]

Without such a progress in autonomy, we will continue to live lives entirely devoted to accumulation or to frivolous consumption, and societies will continue to race towards the cliff edge: we will pursue a quest that is both infinite and purposeless.

It is in that sense that limits can become a source of freedom. The ecological wall leaves us no choice: we must change. This obligation imposed on us, however, is also the opportunity for each of us to gain in reflexivity – to re-examine what we truly want. And at a societal level, it is an invitation to broaden our political imagination, to invent new ways in which to realize a society of equals and to combat precarity and social exclusion.

*   *   *

This short text has its immediate origin in the meeting I had with Pope Francis at the Vatican, in September 2022. I had been asked to propose a diagnosis of global poverty and to identify certain levers that could be used to eradicate it. I am grateful to the organizers of this meeting for having thus provided me with the necessary motivation to summarize, in these pages, the spirit in which I am fulfilling my role as the UN Special Rapporteur on extreme poverty and human rights.

Olivier De Schutter
September 2023

Abbreviations

CBN	cost of basic needs
CESCR	Committee on Economic, Social and Cultural Rights
EROI	Energy return on investment
ETS	emissions trading system
GDP	gross domestic product
HLPE	high-level panel of experts
ILO	International Labour Organization
IPBES	Intergovernmental Science-Policy Platform on Biodiversity and Ecosystem Services
IRP	International Resource Panel
PPP	parity purchasing power
UN	United Nations
UNCTAD	United Nations Conference for Trade and Development

Introduction

Sarita, a woman living in poverty, once told me:

> We must keep our heads down: we are humiliated and
> exploited. We sacrifice everything, we constantly have to
> fight. But society puts obstacles in our way. We remain
> marked, marked because we are poor. It is a burden we bear,
> from generation to generation. A vicious circle.

Sarita lives in Peru. In Colombia, not far from her home
country, it takes eleven generations before a person born in
poverty is able to earn the country's average income. In Argentina, no less than six generations would be needed to efface the
burden of poverty, and nine generations would be required in
South Africa or in Brazil.[1] Indeed, in some emerging countries
such as Brazil, 70 per cent of the average individual's earn-
ings can be attributed to earning differences between fathers,
that carry on to the children: poverty is perpetuated from one
generation to the next because we seem unable to break the
vicious cycles that reduce life chances for children born in
low-income households.[2]

But the call I make here is not only about Peru, Colombia, Argentina or South Africa. And it is not just about Sarita.
It is about the unbearable struggle of hundreds of millions
of people to survive in a world that has never been wealthier, more abundant or more opulent. It is about poverty in the
midst of prosperity. It is about the slow yet steady and constant efforts of families who face humiliation and exploitation

to ensure a better future for their children, despite the obstacles and setbacks they face.

To these households, general economic progress has meant little in their everyday lives. In the years prior to Brexit, an expert addressed a British audience seeking to convince them that their country should not leave the European Union because it would result in a loss in GDP. In that room, one woman stood up and shouted: 'That's your bloody GDP! It's not ours!'[3]

This reaction is understandable. The rising tide of growth, particularly in wealthy countries, has failed to lift all boats equally. In Britain, where the median income has risen by 2.2 per cent on average over the last five years, the poorest fifth of the country has seen their income *fall* by 1.6 per cent.[4]

Deprivation is thus perpetuated from generation to generation while those who are better off disproportionately reap the benefits of economic growth. The gap between the rich and the poor has widened. These developments have now become a major concern. There is near unanimity about the urgent need to address poverty and inequality. Divergences persist, however, with regard to how to do so. Indeed, how to define poverty and how to eradicate it are as contested as the need to act swiftly and boldly is widely recognized.

With this short contribution, I hope to achieve three objectives. First, I seek to distinguish different understandings of poverty. In particular, I contrast poverty as defined by experts focused on the satisfaction of basic needs in a range of areas (including standards of living) with the lived experience of people in poverty, who are more concerned with the social exclusion they face as a result of being poor than with (solely) avoiding destitution. 'Modern' poverty is the inability of the individual to meet the expectations of the society in which they live. It is not an absolute notion, and certainly not limited to the satisfaction of physiological needs. It is a relative notion, related to social norms and to the gap between the poor and the rich that causes social exclusion.

Second, I aim to illustrate the limitations of the conventional approach to poverty eradication, which sees creating wealth as a condition for redistribution. There is no doubt that growth, understood as an increase in the value of economic output,[5] is still much needed in poor countries, provided it helps to satisfy the most pressing needs. However, the obsessive quest for growth comes at a huge cost, that we cannot afford to ignore.[6] Nor does growth contribute to reducing poverty if it is not equitably spread: it can even widen the gap between rich and poor, thus worsening 'modern' poverty instead of providing the tools necessary to combat it. Indeed, the widening of this gap between the richest and the poorest segments of the population, in particular in the countries boasting the fastest economic growth, should be a major source of concern in the global effort to eradicate poverty. And in rich countries, it has been many years since growth has become counter-productive: it does not contribute to improved well-being, it 'modernizes' poverty without eliminating it, and it puts an unbearable pressure on the Earth's ability to provide resources and to absorb waste and pollution.

An effort in imagination is therefore required. We must move beyond the mainstream view that sees growth as the key to eradicating poverty. Indeed, my third objective is to open a dialogue about the tools that could be used to combat 'modern' poverty. Social movements and civil society groups are already seeking to develop such tools, in a still largely experimentalist mode. They are joining forces with unions and environmental NGOs in a search for new pathways to development. Academics are also entering into the debate, searching for 'prosperity without growth'.[7] New alliances are emerging, that were impossible to imagine even ten years ago, gradually coalescing to create a powerful 'counter-movement' to the dominant narrative of progress. Its message: we must cease treating the world and human beings as mere resources to create wealth and increase profits, even under the guise of combating poverty. As an attempt to rethink the fight against poverty without growth, this book is a modest contribution to this collective effort.

1

What is Poverty?

There exists a conventional definition of poverty, and there is a conventional view as to how to address it. Both are connected.

The conventional definition is that poverty is about a lack of sufficient income to meet the necessities of life. And the conventional response to date, based on this money-centric understanding of poverty, has been that incomes should be raised. By growing the economy, it should be possible to create jobs and raise the necessary public revenue to finance public services and social protection, thus overcoming the scourge of poverty by improving income security for those at the bottom end of income earners. Provided the incomes of those in poverty rise enough to allow them to move above a certain poverty line, we are told, poverty will be eradicated.

The money-centric approach to poverty

This is the approach underlying Sustainable Development Goal 1 (SDG1), adopted as part of the 2030 Agenda for Sustainable Development. Under SDG1, governments have pledged to eradicate extreme poverty by 2030 and, according to the official narrative, significant progress has already been made towards this target.

Between 1990 and 2015 the number of people in extreme poverty decreased from 1.9 billion to 736 million, and from 36 per cent to 10 per cent of the world's population. The historical decline of poverty continued between 2015 and 2018, with 656 million people in extreme poverty in 2018, and the global poverty rate falling to 8.6 per cent. According to the *Sustainable Development Goals Report 2022*, progress would have continued if it hadn't been suddenly interrupted by the Covid-19 pandemic, which resulted in at least 75 million more people falling into extreme poverty.[1]

Yet, despite these figures, what we need here is more humility, not self-congratulation.[2] The victory claims noted above are conveniently based on the international poverty line used by the World Bank, of US $1.90 per day in 2011 (in purchasing power parity [PPP] dollars). This line is so low, however, that even those who do not fall under the threshold may be barely able to survive, let alone live in dignity. It corresponds to 1.41 euros per day in Portugal, 7.49 yuan per day in China, 22.49 pesos per day in Mexico, or 355.18 naira per day in Nigeria. No one can seriously contend that anybody can lead a decent life at or just above such levels of income.

The scorecard is even less impressive once you consider that most people who, over the past thirty years, have been raised above the international poverty line, are now just above that line. That they are able to escape starvation, thanks to a combination of some income and of various solidarity networks, cannot plausibly mean that they have overcome poverty.

Moreover, the successes the international community boasts in the reduction of poverty have much to do with developments in a single country: China, which has succeeded in reducing poverty from 750 million people in 1990 to 10 million in 2015, and which claims it has succeeded in eradicating extreme poverty entirely since 2021. Indeed, leaving out China, the number of people living below $2.50 per day would barely have changed between 1990 and 2015; it would in fact have *increased* by 140 million people in sub-Saharan Africa and the Middle East. It is difficult to see any cause for celebration here.

6

Under SDG1 therefore, the bar is set so low that it is essentially meaningless as a measure of poverty. The international poverty line of $1.90 per day, used until recently to measure extreme poverty across low-income countries, essentially replicates the initial approaches of thirty years ago, when a team at the World Bank took a subset of the poorest countries and compared their poverty lines to extract the 'absolute' component of such lines. In other terms, what is needed not to starve.[3] We end up setting the ambition for the international community so low that progress towards reaching SDG1 is practically built in to how success is measured.[4]

The international poverty line was updated in 2022 to $2.15 per day in 2017 US dollars, a change that roughly corresponds to the inflation that had happened since the $1.90 measure was established. The problem lies deeper, however, than simply the level at which the threshold of 'poverty' is set. The real issue is whether approaching poverty by focusing on the level of income needed to meet the essential needs is justified.

According to this approach, sometimes referred to as the 'cost of basic needs' (CBN) approach, individuals are deemed poor if their income is insufficient to meet the costs of a basket of food and non-food items considered essential to be an active participant in society.[5] The limitations of the CBN approach have long been recognized, however.[6] First, even people who do not starve and who have a roof over their heads can experience poverty if they are unable to meet certain social expectations, such as providing a decent funeral for their parents or a wedding for their children.[7] The great sociologist Peter Townsend, working in the context of the United Kingdom, defined his approach to poverty as this:

> Individuals, families and groups in the population can be said to be in poverty when they lack the resources to obtain the type of diet, participate in the activities and have the

living conditions and the amenities which are customary, or at least widely encouraged or approved in the societies to which they belong. Their resources are so seriously below those commanded by the average family that they are in effect excluded from ordinary patterns, customs and activities.[8]

Second, the ability of each person to 'convert' income into effective freedom (or the expansion of capabilities, in the terminology of Amartya K. Sen)[9] differs widely from individual to individual, depending on one's personal characteristics and needs. The level of income required to sustain a decent life may have to be set higher for a person with a disability, for a person whose health requires costly medical treatments, or for a person lacking the social networks or extended family relationships that would allow them to withstand economic shocks, than for individuals who are physically fit and can count on such forms of inter-personal solidarity. Similarly, the situation of people in rural areas can differ markedly from that of people in urban settings, because the cost of transportation will be higher for the first group while the prices of basic commodities may be lower than in cities, for instance.

Third, the level of income required to lead a decent life, allowing the individual not only to meet their basic needs but also to avoid social exclusion – the shame and stigma that result from one's inability to meet social expectations – depends on which goods and services are allocated on the basis of one's ability to pay. In societies where education and healthcare are free, for example, or where subsidized housing is available for low-income earners, lower incomes may still allow for the enjoyment of social rights, whereas in societies not providing such public goods, higher incomes will be necessary to meet the necessities of life.

The multidimensional approach to poverty

This is why, since the mid-1990s, poverty has been defined as a multidimensional phenomenon, including but not reducible to low income.[10] This multidimensional approach sees poverty as both the cause and the outcome of a range of deprivations, covering the full range of human rights – whether civil, cultural, economic, political or social. The Programme of Action adopted at the 1995 World Summit for Social Development states that:

> Poverty has various manifestations, including lack of income and productive resources sufficient to ensure sustainable livelihoods; hunger and malnutrition; ill health; limited or lack of access to education and other basic services; increased morbidity and mortality from illness; homelessness and inadequate housing; unsafe environments; and social discrimination and exclusion. It is also characterized by a lack of participation in decision-making and in civil, social and cultural life.[11]

Human rights bodies have taken a similar view. In a statement adopted in 2001, the Committee on Economic, Social and Cultural Rights (CESCR) defined poverty as:

> A human condition characterized by sustained or chronic deprivation of the resources, capabilities, choices, security and power necessary for the enjoyment of an adequate standard of living and other civil, cultural, economic, political and social rights.[12]

The finding on which the multidimensional approach to poverty is based is simple enough: people in poverty not only face numerous obstacles in accessing their rights and entitlements (including education, housing, nutritious food, healthcare, and work, but also political participation),[13] they are also are caught in a vicious cycle in which those deprivations themselves make it more difficult for them to escape poverty. It is therefore only by addressing the full range of deprivations, rather than income poverty alone, that significant progress will be achieved in the fight against poverty.

The one considerable advantage of approaching poverty as a multidimensional phenomenon is that the set of policy measures used to address poverty goes beyond tools that simply increase income. As long as poverty is defined as a lack of income, poverty will be combated by a combination of tax and subsidies, the ultimate aim of which is to improve the purchasing power of the individual: active labour market policies and minimum wage legislation, progressive taxation and social security benefits, all converge towards that end. Once, however, you consider that poverty – understood in a multidimensional perspective as a set of deprivations in a range of areas – can be tackled not only by measures strengthening the income security of the individual, but also by the provision of public goods, policies such as improved access to social housing, universal and free access to pre-school and secondary education (beyond the minimum requirement of free primary education) or universal and free healthcare (beyond the minimum duty to provide life-saving treatment), are enrolled in the fight against poverty and can serve to reduce the poverty count.

The modern face of poverty

The multidimensional approach to poverty presents its own limitations, however. One is methodological. Achievements in areas such as health, education or standard of living can be quantified to some extent with the use of the right indicators. The qualitative dimensions of the services provided in order to allow people to escape poverty may be more difficult to capture, however, and there is a risk that, once indicators are used, efforts focus on improving on such indicators, rather than on those qualitative dimensions that the indicators do not incorporate or incorporate only weakly. You can measure the school enrolment rate of children, whether boys benefit more than girls, or compare average number of years of schooling across groups; but not whether the educational system performs well in training children in critical thinking or even in ensuring that pupils master the essential skills. You can put a figure on the ratio of medical doctors to the population; not so much on how well patients are treated by the doctors that they see.

Two other limitations are even more significant. The first is that the lived experience of people in poverty is not just about a lack of income, nor is it simply about a lack of access to certain goods or services that would allow them to lead a decent life, in which their basic needs are met. It is about social exclusion, discrimination, and social or institutional maltreatment.

The more affluent societies become, the more such social exclusion has its source in the modernization of poverty: a phenomenon through which – even when the basic needs of the individual are satisfied – those living on low incomes remain socially excluded because social expectations rise with the increase in general affluence. In all but the poorest countries today, you are considered to be poor when you cannot afford a mobile phone, when you have no access to the internet, when you cannot face catastrophic expenditures following events such as the loss of a job or an illness, or, as already noted when you cannot organize a decent funeral for your parents or a wedding for your children.

Poverty is not just the result of being unable to satisfy basic needs – it is the result of being unable to meet the expectations of neighbours or family. It is not an absolute notion – it is relative to the standard of living of others. It cannot be addressed solely by providing individuals with a minimum set of guarantees, by placing a roof over their heads or by putting food on their plates: it can only be tackled by combating the gaps between the richest and the poorest, and thus the social exclusion that results from social comparisons.

Social psychologists note that we attach more importance to our position in comparison to others against whom we rank ourselves, than to our absolute levels of consumption alone.[14] Modern poverty is about the sense of exclusion that stems from such comparisons. It is, moreover, not about income alone, but also about social affiliation and recognition. When people in poverty are asked what poverty means to them, they spontaneously refer to the humiliation and negative stereotyping they face in a number of settings: in their search for a job or for an apartment; in their interactions with schoolteachers or healthcare providers; or in their encounters with social workers and administrations.

These daily experiences of discrimination and social and institutional maltreatment contribute to the vicious cycles in which people in poverty are trapped. Social discrimination was a major theme in the *Voices of the Poor* study of 2000,[15] and 'social maltreatment' is one of the 'hidden dimensions of poverty' highlighted in a study conducted jointly by Oxford University and ATD Fourth World using the 'Merging of Knowledge' methodology involving people in poverty.[16] In this study, 'social maltreatment' is described as 'the way in which people in poverty are typically treated within and by the community', often facing stereotyping, blame and stigma. 'The process of othering is commonplace [where] people in poverty are thought to be different in kind and socially inferior, engaging in disreputable behaviour either as a cause or a result of their poverty'.[17] Social maltreatment in turn feeds institutional maltreatment or abuse, defined as 'the common failure of public and private institutions to respond appropriately to the circumstances, needs and aspirations of people in poverty'.[18]

A final limitation of the multidimensional approach to poverty as a combination of deprivations is that, as long as poverty is defined as access to certain goods or services, whether provided by the market (on the basis of purchasing power) or by the collective (in the form of public goods), poverty reduction will be perceived – implicitly and, more often than not, explicitly – as depending on economic growth.

It is here that the conventional understanding of how poverty is to be defined supports a conventional understanding of how it is to be defeated. As long as poverty is defined as a lack of access to certain things, the solution to eradicating it is to provide more of those things, at a more affordable price or even for free. This requires growth, understood as an increase in the GDP per capita, and therefore of total monetary wealth. This is the current orthodoxy.

2

Is Economic Growth
the Solution?

The idea that poverty reduction requires economic growth seems intuitive. It fits neatly within mainstream macroeconomic debates between the fiscally conservative, often found to the right of the political spectrum, and those, coming more often from the left, who argue for demand-driven solutions. For the former group, fiscal consolidation is a precondition for sustainable economic growth over the long-term. For the latter, austerity kills growth, and it is only by raising the incomes of lower-income earners and the middle class that output will be stimulated to increase and investors to invest. While seemingly opposed to one another, however, both views in fact converge on the essentials. They argue about which pathway is best to stimulate growth. But both agree that growth is needed.

The reign of this orthodoxy can be readily explained. In order to redistribute wealth and thus alleviate poverty, there must first be wealth created to redistribute. Moreover, growth is generally seen to hold the promise of employment creation. Since poverty cannot be tackled by social protection alone, but requires that the active population be provided with jobs – allowing in turn for their income from work to be taxed and their social contributions to finance insurance schemes such as unemployment benefits and old-age pensions – growth seems to be indispensable to any successful poverty-reduction programme. Indeed, in the absence of growth, the increased labour productivity allowed by technological advances would result in massive under-employment: the economy must grow, and both output and consumption must rise, if we want to avoid large portions of the workforce becoming redundant.

This is the conventional wisdom. The Sustainable Development Agenda endorsed at the highest level in 2015 confirms the attractiveness of growth as a means, if not *the* means, to overcome our predicament.[1] Indeed, the idea is so well established that any suggestion that poverty reduction could be achieved without growth is immediately denounced as eccentric to the extreme.

This conviction, however, is profoundly disabling. It restricts the imagination, discouraging the search for solutions beyond growth. Indeed, in the current context, in which a number of factors, both structural and more conjunctural, impede the ability of economies to achieve growth, it is tempting to believe that there is nothing more we can do, in the short term at least, than to put all our energy into trying to relaunch growth, whatever the human and ecological costs – since no anti-poverty effort can succeed without it. But is this devotion to growth justified? Must growth be seen as the precondition of everything else?

False universality

Perhaps most striking about pro-growth arguments is the contrast between the universality of the prescription and the specificity of each region. Growth is said to be the remedy for all, as if the needs of rich countries were the same as those of poor countries; as if those of countries with a stagnant or even a declining population were similar to those of countries with a fast-growing population; and as if growth in highly unequal countries meant the same thing as growth in more equal countries.

We should be weary of universal prescriptions. How credible are remedies that gloss over such differences, as if they didn't matter? Shouldn't we care whether growth – the increase in economic output, measured in monetary terms – will allow already rich populations to buy more cars, or to fly more frequently, or whether it will allow poor populations to eat more diverse diets and send their children to school, rather than condemning them to work in the fields with their parents? Shouldn't we care whether growth will simply allow wealthy populations to grow wealthier in places where the size of the population remains the same, or whether it will instead allow individuals to maintain their existing standard of living, by allowing the economy to absorb the growing work-force that results from fast population growth? Shouldn't we care whether growth will serve primarily to further enrich the richest groups within the population, or whether it will benefit primarily those at the bottom?

Both the nature of economic growth and its desirability should depend on the circumstances of each country. As a universal recipe for poverty reduction, it is barely plausible.

Such universalistic approaches also hide important questions of equity. We cannot ignore, for instance, that while most of the population growth since the 1950s has been in non-OECD (Organisation for Economic Co-operation and Development) countries, the rise in consumption is still largely dominated by OECD countries. In other words, growth in relatively poor countries can be plausibly presented as a means to provide opportunities for a fast-growing work-force and to allow households to achieve standards of living that bring them closer to those of the richer populations of the global North; but neither of these justifications hold for countries that are already rich.

In higher-income countries, growth has chiefly allowed already rich populations to become richer still, and to create the impression that all groups within those populations will one day be able to mimic the lifestyles of the wealthiest segments among them (an illusory dream that does not weaken its hold on the imagination, and a point to which I return to later).

There is a reason, however, why we still speak of growth as a remedy for all world regions. It is because, in a strongly interconnected world economy, how one region fares has a significant impact on the other regions with which it trades. Stagnation or recession in advanced economies in particular, means fewer opportunities for economies in poorer regions to make progress, where this progress relies on the possibility of exporting to consumers of rich countries who have a superior ability to pay. It is in that sense that growth in the global North supports growth in the global South, and may support poor countries' efforts to improve the well-being of their populations.

The argument is limited in two ways, however. First, it underestimates the costs of export-led development, even in the low-income countries that most need to increase their monetary wealth. Such a form of development typically is extractivist in nature, because of the distance between production and consumption – between where the resources are and people are exploited, and where the final products are consumed. Where such a distance exists, the end-consumers are typically less concerned about the impacts of their choices: they will prioritize price above everything else and since they are not connected to the communities that bear the impacts of the production process, they will care less about the consequences. (The recent proliferation of labels and supply chain monitoring initiatives to counteract this distancing merely confirms the reality of the problem.)

Moreover, export-led development is generally highly unequal. Those who succeed are those who can be competitive in global supply chains thanks to their ability to achieve economies of scale and to produce to the required standards, often using technologies or methods of production imposed on them by the buyers. Many others fail. The result is increased concentration of power, particularly in the hands of large buyers – the traders and the brands that act as gatekeepers to high-value markets. At the same time large suppliers are better placed to seize the opportunities of globalization than smaller-size suppliers. Hence buyer power grows, and competition between suppliers increases, leading to further imbalances in supply chains.

The modernization of agrifood supply chains is typical in this regard. Large retailers today tend to prefer to source from large wholesalers and large processing firms. This leads to what has been called a 'mutually reinforcing dual consolidation':[2] by sourcing from larger wholesalers and processors, retailers reduce transaction costs and have access to a diversity of product types in a 'one-stop shop'; the invoicing system is formalized, allowing the retailers to discharge their accounting obligations for value-added tax accounting and product liability; and the packaging and branding of products is superior to that which smaller processors or wholesalers would be able to achieve.[3] In addition, large buyers can obtain from the sellers a number of concessions that reflect their dominant buyer power, such as discounts from the market price that reflect the savings made by the seller due to increased production, or the passing on to the seller of certain costs associated with functions normally carried out by the buyer, such as grading of the livestock or stocking of shelves. This not only makes it more attractive for the retailers to source from these dominant buyers, since they may benefit from this superior buyer power that such larger suppliers have. It also further strengthens the position of the dominant buyers, who can acquire a competitive advantage over less dominant buyers in the downstream markets, leading to the acquisition by the larger agribusiness firms of dominance on both the buying and selling markets.[4] These mechanisms are therefore self-reinforcing: buyer power grows by the very fact of being exercised, and the expansion of global supply chains results in an increased concentration in the food production and distribution chains.[5]

Export-led development thus has a tendency to magnify inequalities, as bigness is a competitive advantage in itself. Moreover, even if the expansion of export opportunities were essential to the development of poor countries at least at a macro level, this does not necessarily mean that growth in the global North should be pursued as a development tool. The proper answer to this predicament is not to entertain a false sense of universality as regards development pathways. It is instead to promote more regional integration and South–South trade, rather than to insist on global integration and on long supply chains. And to encourage achieving progress by stimulating domestic demand and raising standards of living for people in poverty in the global South, rather than by pushing for producers from less developed regions to serve the high-value markets of the global North. The priority should be to improve access to markets for producers from the global South, particularly small-scale producers, by increasing the incomes of the local populations within those countries; not to push those producers to cater to the demand and requirements of consumers in the global North.

The limits of growth

As a means to improve well-being, growth also promises more than it can deliver.

The promise of growth is that, by increasing production, the needs of all members of society will gradually be met, and no one will be left wanting. This approach explains the continued focus on GDP growth as a measure of progress. It now appears overly optimistic, however, and even astonishingly naive. As Richard Easterlin has noted, increases in GDP have been disconnected from improvements in subjective well-being in the advanced economies since the early 1970s. Beyond a certain point of material opulence and comfort across society, he noted, additional improvements do not contribute to an improvement in subjective perceptions of well-being, or what most people call happiness.[6]

One major reason for this gap is that GDP growth only provides an indication of the wealth created in the economy as a whole. It is silent about how such wealth is distributed. Yet the staggering rise of inequalities in all societies since the mid-1980s results in a situation in which, for most people, the proud announcement by political leaders that GDP has increased under their watch (and, of course, thanks to the policies they have put in place) is entirely unrelated to their everyday lived experience. If not combined with a reduction in inequalities, for the vast majority of households in most societies of the world, GDP growth bears little or no relationship to the increase of their own purchasing power, and thus to the improvement of their material living conditions.[7]

There is another and more subtle reason why growth promises more than it can deliver. The reason is that even while economic growth increases overall material opulence, it shapes new desires and brings about new forms of dissatisfaction. That is true for the subjective feeling of happiness, but it is equally true for poverty understood as social exclusion – and therefore how an individual fares relative to others: an overall improvement of access to material goods or services will not remedy social exclusion if social expectations rise even faster, leading the individuals who cannot meet such expectations to feel excluded. This is how a *general* rise of affluence within society not only can go hand in hand with, but may even worsen, the *individual* experience of being left behind.

This is the counter-productivity of growth.[8] The more certain items are produced at scale and enjoyed by a larger part of the population, the more they become indispensable for all. Not being able to access those items leads naturally to feelings of exclusion. It is in that sense that growth can increase modern poverty.

With his usual lucidity, Keynes distinguished in this regard two classes among the needs of human beings: 'those needs which are absolute in the sense that we feel them whatever the situation of our fellow human beings may be, and those which are relative only in that their satisfaction lifts us above, makes us feel superior to, our fellows'. He remarked that the needs of the second class, the 'relative' needs, which result from the desire to keep up with the neighbours or even to jump ahead of them, 'may indeed be insatiable; for the higher the general level the higher still are they'.[9] The result is what John Kenneth Galbraith, another great economist of the past century, called the 'Dependence Effect': while it is ostensibly meant to satisfy pre-existing needs, production creates new needs, as what was once the privilege of a happy few becomes a legitimate expectation for all to acquire and to enjoy.[10]

This is why the persistence of wealth and income inequalities largely cancel out the positive impacts on well-being that are expected to derive from an increase in GDP. In response to the invitation of French President Nicolas Sarkozy to work on new indicators of well-being, the Stiglitz Commission on the Measurement of Economic Performance and Social Progress noted that the failure to value the reduction of inequality appropriately in our classic measures of progress could explain, in part, the gap between official statistics focusing on the aggregate level of performance of the economy and the subjective perception of well-being:

> When there are large changes in inequality (more generally a change in income distribution), gross domestic product (GDP) or any other aggregate computed per capita may not provide an accurate assessment of the situation in which most people find themselves. If inequality increases enough relative to the increase in average per capital GDP, most people can be worse off even though average income is increasing.[11]

Even if the situation of a particular individual improves in *absolute* terms, but remains stagnant (or, even worse, falls) *in relation to other members of society*, that individual may experience a loss in well-being that his or her increased purchasing power, and thus the improvement in material conditions, may not compensate for. This goes a long way towards explaining the paradox highlighted by Easterlin: one reason why GDP growth in high-income countries has become unrelated to measures of subjective well-being may be that, unless it is combined with greater equality, income growth is a 'zero-sum game'. Growth in average incomes that leaves people far apart from one another hardly satisfies their desire to compare favourably to those around them, and so gains in life satisfaction are, at best, minimal.[12]

The only gain, in fact, is in what Albert Hirschman and Michael Rothschild have called the 'tunnel effect': just as a car driver, when stuck in a traffic jam, may experience some solace from finding that the lane next to theirs is moving forward, some people may experience an increase in 'happiness' from seeing others around them in wealthier positions, because they anticipate that their turn will come next.[13] The intuition of Hirschman and Rothschild has been confirmed since by empirical studies highlighting the psychological comfort one obtains from projected gains. Contrary to what standard economic analysis might have anticipated (in which future gains are more or less heavily discounted), most subjects appear to prefer to move from the least pleasurable to the most pleasurable experiences, because the very anticipation of future improvement is highly valued as a source of subjective well-being.[14] Indeed, this may be the only explanation for the tolerance of much of the public for very high levels of inequality: the reason why inequalities are not denounced even more strongly as a major scandal may be that people believe they, in turn, will be able to climb to the top.[15]

The overwhelming evidence is that people care not only about *absolute* income, allowing them to acquire what they need to lead a decent life, but also about *relative* income, and the 'tunnel effect' noted by Hirschman and Rothschild would barely compensate for the social comparisons and dissatisfaction brought about by inequality. This is at the heart of the rat race that is so characteristic of our competitive society: if people want to be able to acquire what will allow them to distinguish themselves from their fellow citizens, they will have to be richer than them.[16] Indeed, as general affluence increases, larger portions of households' budgets go to the acquisition of goods that are positional in nature. Such goods are sought after because they allow individuals to distinguish themselves from others, and to claim a certain rank within society. But once a large part of the population has access to such goods, the reward disappears: my impressive-looking car is of much lesser value to me if I am in a society in which the vast majority have equally impressive cars.[17] The benefits expected from the progress of material wealth, and from its extension to all groups of society thanks to mass production, thus end up cancelling themselves out.

The race for more never ends. It is a race, moreover, that is deeply frustrating for all who engage in it – in fact, for all members of society, with the exception of the ascetic. This is not only because, as noted, the signpost signalling the finish line is constantly being shifted further away. It is also because the items that one aspires to as productivity improves and as incomes increase, thus making these items more affordable, systematically disappoint once they are acquired.

Our brains want not just comfort, but excitement. It is not enough that all our needs be satisfied – we also want the pleasure that comes from moving from one state to another. While accelerating from 20 km/hr to 80 km/hr may provide that pleasure, driving along a highway at the constant speed of 80 km/hr is boring. So it is with consumer items: people crave novelty, and they will not be satisfied simply once all their needs are met.[18] Indeed, this was how Albert Hirschman (yes, Hirschman again) explained our tolerance for planned obsolescence – when short lifespans are deliberately built into the products we buy. If we continue to accept we have to change phones every three years and buy a new car every ten years, instead of demanding from producers that they provide goods that are much more resistant and repairable, might it not have something to do with the fact that while durable consumer goods with long lifespans provide a certain level of 'comfort', they only offer a single shot of 'pleasure'?[19] The language of toxicology here it not only metaphoric: endocrinologists have recently documented what they describe as a true addiction to what is novel and brings about new forms of excitement.[20]

The limits of growth are thus becoming increasingly clear. The long-held belief that the flourishing of each member of society depends on the constant expansion of the possibilities of material consumption is now less plausible than ever.[21] On the contrary, by increasing social expectations, the rise of overall affluence within a society may in fact increase modern poverty: the sense of exclusion one experiences when it becomes impossible to meet the rising standards of what makes you feel a full member of the community. It is high time, therefore, that we launch a debate on the orthodox view that well-being correlates to opportunities for material consumption. In advanced societies, we should seek to identify sources of subjective well-being and instruments to fight against social exclusion that do not require the further pursuit of growth.

This is all the more urgent as we are now coming to understand that the infinite pursuit of growth is incompatible with the limited biocapacity of our planet; in other words, with the ability of our ecosystems to continue to provide the resources we extract from them, or to absorb the pollution we produce to increase economic output.

It is the belief that well-being depends on increases in material consumption that makes it appear so imperative to strive for an increase in income combined with a reduction of the real price of consumer items: the standardization of production, the increased competition between producers, and market-led technological innovations, all of which are intended to create the conditions for mass consumption, have no other justification. This belief is now increasingly discredited. But it has been powerful enough to have already had devastating impacts on the environment.

The Earth's boundaries

ENVIRONMENTAL DESTRUCTION AND POVERTY

The lucid observer will not fail to note this paradox: while the orthodoxy presents growth as the precondition for poverty alleviation wherever poverty persists, the further destruction of the ecosystems that growth necessarily entails is the most significant threat to people in poverty worldwide. This is another source of the counter-productivity of growth.

The rise of mass consumption society and globalization have resulted, since the 1950s, in what scientists have called the 'Great Acceleration'.[22] People in poverty, among which minority groups are over-represented, have benefited to a certain extent from the lowering of the prices of consumer items. But they have also been disproportionately affected by the negative impacts of this acceleration.

People in poverty are the most immediately and the most seriously affected by environmental degradation. They are the first victims of air pollution, because they generally live closer to the sources of pollution[23] and because they live in small, overcrowded dwellings that are more difficult to ventilate properly.[24] They are the most at risk from landslides or flooding, because they are forced to live wherever they can afford housing.[25] As recalled by the Chennai Guidance for the integration of biodiversity and poverty eradication, elaborated within the Convention on Biological Diversity,[26] they are also more dependent on ecosystems for their livelihoods.[27] Globally, 1.2 billion jobs (40 per cent of total world employment), most of which are in Africa and Asia and the Pacific, rely directly on the effective management and sustainability of a healthy environment.[28] People in poverty, including the 476 million Indigenous peoples,[29] are therefore the most affected by climate disruptions.[30] How credible, then, are poverty eradication strategies that destroy the very foundations of the livelihoods of people in poverty, albeit in the name of creating wealth?

THE UNFULFILLED PROMISE OF 'GREEN GROWTH'

Of course, some would argue that growth does not necessarily have to lead us to cross planetary boundaries – the thresholds of resource extraction and pollution beyond which we leave the 'safe space' within which humanity can operate.[31] This is the promise of 'green growth', on which the 2012 Rio+20 Conference on Sustainable Development and its outcome document, *The Future We Want*, place so much emphasis. The promise is that economic growth can be combined with a reduction of its ecological footprint, such footprint being calculated combining resource use and pollution.[32] The 'green economy', we are told, is one which 'should contribute to eradicating poverty as well as sustained economic growth, enhancing social inclusion, improving human welfare and creating opportunities for employment and decent work for all, while maintaining the healthy functioning of the Earth's ecosystems'.[33]

These objectives are certainly worth supporting. But can they be attained, *through growth*? The data suggest not. In 2019, Jason Hickel and Giorgos Kallis provided a meticulous and systematic review of the empirical evidence.[34] Their review confirmed that, through most of the twentieth century, resource use increased at a slower pace than did GDP. This demonstrates *relative decoupling* between economic growth and resource use, made possible thanks to the use of more efficient technologies and a certain dematerialization of the economy. Yet, apart from the fact that this improvement did not last,[35] it is not *absolute decoupling*. Although resource consumption increased more slowly than GDP, it has not been decreasing.

It has sometimes been alleged that European countries, at least, have achieved such absolute decoupling. But this is a myth based solely on an accounting illusion. The impression of absolute decoupling is created when taking into account *domestic* material consumption alone. Yet, once the resource use implied in imports is taken into account, the myth dissolves.[36] In other words, even in the most virtuous European countries, production and consumption patterns have not been transformed to such an extent that they allow for absolute decoupling, once it is considered that Europe has outsourced much of the resource-intensive modes of production that are required to cater to the lifestyles that Europeans continue to entertain.

Even the gradual shift from manufacturing to services does not provide solace. While the provision of services is sometimes perceived as resulting in a 'dematerialization' of growth, reducing the 'throughput' of wealth creation, it requires in fact significant, resource-intensive infrastructure and materials. Moreover, the resource extraction required for a service-based economy, as with industry in general, is increasingly energy-intensive over time because the first resources to be exploited are those that are the easiest and cheapest to extract. The *energy return on investment* (EROI), as it is referred to in ecological economics – in other terms, the ratio of the amount of usable energy that can be produced to the amount of energy expended in the energy production process – thus follows a descending curve: more and more energy must be invested in order to produce the energy needed to keep the economy going. This, combined with the increased levels of consumption favoured by income growth stimulated by a service-based economy, in reality wipes out any apparent benefits that might result from the shift to services.[37]

In order to assess the credibility of the discourse around 'green growth', researchers from the European Environmental Bureau, a large coalition of environmental NGOs, systematically searched for evidence of 'decoupling', both as regards resource use and as regards impacts (including greenhouse gas emissions and biodiversity loss). Their conclusion is this:

[W]e can safely conclude that there is no empirical evidence supporting the existence of [...] an absolute, global, permanent, and sufficiently fast and large decoupling of environmental pressures (both resources and impacts) from economic growth. In the end, our search for robust evidence was unsuccessful, coming up only with a handful of methodologically peculiar exceptions, most often of relative decoupling, and if absolute, mainly temporary and restricted in space, only for territorial indicators (that is to say spatially inconsistent), or having to do with specific local, short-term pollutants. In all cases, the reduction in environmental pressures falls short of current environmental policy targets. After such an extensive search, it is safe to say that the type of decoupling acclaimed by green growth advocates is essentially a statistical figment.[38]

This finding allowed these researchers, in their concluding section, to bid 'farewell to green growth'. Technological advances simply cannot compensate for the destructive nature of our consumption patterns.

One important nuance should be added to this picture, however. For there is one area where *absolute* decoupling, even considered on a 'consumption base' rather than in a 'territory-based' approach, has in fact started to occur: it is the area of greenhouse gas emissions. Only a few years ago, the consensus among researchers was that greenhouse gas emissions had only been reduced on a territorial basis in advanced economies thanks to a slowdown of the economy and the outsourcing of the most polluting industries, combined with an increase in imports from countries where emissions were allowed to increase.[39] The most recent assessments are however more optimistic. In 2023, Jefim Vogel and Jason Hickel reviewed the performance of 36 OECD jurisdictions during the period 2013–19, deliberately reading the available evidence in the light which is the most favourable to the hypothesis of green growth. They found that eleven countries had managed to achieve absolute decoupling during that period. This period (2013–19) is situated between the great financial crisis and the Covid-19 pandemic: the assessment focuses, therefore, not on times of exceptional economic recessions, but instead on a period of normal growth (or even of stronger-than-usual growth, during a period of economic recovery). Vogel and Hickel add an important proviso to their conclusions, however: while clean technologies (including the increased proportion of renewables in the energy mix) did allow absolute decoupling to occur in those eleven jurisdictions, the speed at which this is taking place is too slow for us to remain within the carbon budget resulting from the 2015 Paris Agreement, taking into account equity considerations. Based on their decoupling achievements during the period considered, the eleven jurisdictions that achieved absolute decoupling of greenhouse gas emissions from GDP growth would require 223 years on average 'to reduce their respective 2022 emissions by 95 per cent', by the end of which period they 'would [have burned] between five times and 162 times (on average, 27 times) their respective remaining post-2022 national fair-shares of the global carbon budget for 1.5°C in the process'.[40] In other terms: the decarbonization of the economy is occurring, but it is certainly not occurring at the speed required, and we would be foolish therefore to invest too many hopes in this development – not least because similar instances of absolute decoupling are not occurring with regard to the other major ecological crises, such as biodiversity loss and resource use.

Nor is the insufficiency of technology itself the sole culprit. Three additional factors explain why the race is unequal between consumption and technological advances.

The first is the so-called 'rebound effect'.[41] Increased efficiency in production methods, allowing for instance for the reduction of the amount of energy per output (per distance travelled, per surface heated, per volume produced), may lead to an increase in consumption, because the good or the service will be cheaper. This is known as the 'substitution effect'. Moreover, efficiency-enhancing technologies may allow consumers to save money, leading them to increase their consumption of other products. This is the 'revenue effect'. These effects are particularly significant among low-income groups, in the fields of transport and concerning measures to reduce food waste.[42] But they also are documented when the energy efficiency of dwelling is improved, allowing the household to spend larger parts of its income on other items.[43] Finally, the dissemination of more efficient technologies may lead consumers who (thanks to technological advances) reduce their footprint in certain domains to allow themselves to increase that footprint in other sectors. Studies show, for instance, that carbon credit schemes have led to an increase in airline traffic, because people who otherwise might feel guilty feel that they can ignore the environmental impacts of their travels.[44] And we all know of people around us who travel by air to exotic holiday destinations because they drive a hybrid car during the year, a phenomenon psychologists call the 'compartmentalization effect'.[45] This is the 'licensing effect'. These various effects often operate in combination. Together, they void a significant portion of the gains made from the introduction of more efficient technologies: the total environmental footprint may 'rebound' following the shift to cleaner or greener technologies, sometimes to the point that overall resource use and waste and pollution end up being higher following that shift.

The second factor may be called the 'lock-in' effect. This effect occurs at the more societal level. It refers to the fact that the spread of more efficient technologies may lead to keeping in place systems, including infrastructure, that postpone more structural change. The growing reliance on electric cars, for instance, will help maintain a car-based transportation system, instead of encouraging public transport or cycling options.[46]

Similarly, the introduction of cleaner fuels for airplanes, by bolstering the illusion that, in the future, the continued growth of transport by air can be reconciled with the climate emergency, may justify the building of more airports and discourage the behavioural changes needed to move away from flight-based patterns of travel.[47]

The third factor is the 'middle-class effect'. When average per capita income reaches a certain point (approximately \$6,000 per year), more people can afford to buy consumer items beyond the basic necessities. This in turn spurs growth and leads to the further expansion of the middle class.[48] This point was reached by Egypt in 2011, and by Indonesia, India, the Philippines and Vietnam between 2015 and 2019. It will be reached by Pakistan in 2024 and by Nigeria in 2025. A global middle class is thus emerging, which aspires to replicate the lifestyle of affluent Western countries and now, for the first time, has the means to do so.[49] While the growth concerns some goods and services more than others,[50] the positive feedback between rising incomes, rising consumption and growth cuts across all consumption items. Economists see this as a virtuous cycle. But the impacts are extraordinarily worrisome from the point of view of environmental sustainability. The United Nations International Resource Panel (IRP) estimates that, taking into account the increased consumption resulting from both demographic growth and the rise of a global middle class, we will be consuming three times more resources by 2050 than we did in 2000, even after taking into account the continuation of current patterns of relative resource decoupling thanks to the introduction of cleaner technologies.[51]

From overconsumption to the norm of sufficiency

Consumption is the main factor driving the growth of CO_2 emissions, as well as of the use of raw materials, air pollution, biodiversity loss, nitrogen emissions, and the overuse of scarce water and energy.[52] As might be expected, it is the most affluent households or individuals that have the highest impact on these environmental indicators, for the most part for the satisfaction of desires that have grown entirely unrelated to the satisfaction of their basic needs.

Unlike in the fable of green growth, technology, however much cleaner and greener it becomes, has not been able to compensate for the rise in consumption, let alone for the combination of increased affluence and demographic growth. In 2019, an article titled 'Scientists' warning on affluence' summarized the evidence: 'globally, burgeoning consumption has diminished or cancelled out any gains brought about by technological change aimed at reducing environmental impact'.[53] In the same year, in the study mentioned earlier, the European Environmental Bureau concluded from the empirical evidence reviewed that: 'existing policy strategies aiming to increase efficiency have to be complemented by the pursuit of sufficiency, that is the direct downscaling of economic production in many sectors and parallel reduction of consumption that together will enable the good life within the planet's ecological limits'.[54]

'Sufficiency', thus, should complement the quest for improved 'efficiency', as a means to satisfy needs. 'Sufficiency' refers to lifestyle changes that allow for basic needs to be satisfied, but without overconsumption. Examples of overconsumption include oversized homes or secondary residences for the most affluent; work and leisure patterns that lead to flying or driving over long distances; diets high in animal proteins and processed foods, and that entail large amounts of food waste. Promoting 'sufficiency' also means refocusing business models from providing items that individual consumers own, to providing services in which such items are shared across a larger number of people and in which firms have an interest in repairing items and in ensuring they have a longer life. It means encouraging the sharing of consumer items, as well as the repair and reuse, and, at the end of their life-cycle, the recycling of such items. It means promoting activities that are less energy- and resource-consuming.

The choice for sufficiency-driven lifestyle changes derives from the fundamental question that societies today, which have opted to advance in automatic pilot mode, generally neglect to ask: what do we mean by a good life, and how can we get there? Popular culture, fed with advertising, often portrays the increase in material consumption as a (and mostly *the*) main source of happiness.[55] Materialistic pursuits, however, lead to the neglect of true sources of subjective well-being, including intimate relationships, frequent contacts with nature, and activities that involve 'flow' – activities that engage the mind and are intrinsically motivating, rather than being a means to another end.[56] Such activities, which range from writing to learning a new language, listening to music or walking in a forest, are not only a source of happiness, creating an 'inner glow'; they also have a characteristically low environmental impact.[57] Similarly, plant-based and seasonal diets, and physical activity, including cycling and walking as a substitute for driving, are good both for the planet and for the health of the individual. These lifestyle changes are in the interest of the individual as well as the collective and – because they contribute to minimizing the individual's footprint – future generations.

The alignment between the well-being of the individual and the broader societal interest in the promotion of such lifestyles is an opportunity. It should lead us to avoid the temptation of seeing 'sustainable lifestyles' as a form of sacrifice or renunciation. Indeed, while they are traditionally seen as limiting individual freedoms, lifestyle changes that are based on a norm of sufficiency can be reconceived as acts of autonomy, if agreed to through democratic self-determination. They are an escape from the pressures of social comparison and a way to counteract the manufacturing of desires by the marketing efforts of firms.

As scholars working on 'sustainable consumption corridors' note, self-chosen limits are 'expressions of freedom':

> Exercising restraint by imposing rules upon ourselves is the very essence of autonomy. Viewed this way, the innovative potential of limits becomes visible. Limits can be a powerful creative element, not only in an abstract sense, but also in everyday practices and choices. Often people feel they must sacrifice elements of their current lifestyle in order to make limits work, or they may feel that limits are imposed on them, be it by governments, employers, or others. However, if as individuals and societies, we limit ourselves willingly in pursuit of a larger goal, the imposition of such limits becomes an act of freedom. Limits become a conscious choice to go for something we care about more. That is why such limits should be something we develop through a participatory process. Giving up highly materialistic, overworked and stressed lifestyles, for instance, can be experienced by individuals as freedom to live more authentic lives. Similarly, ecological risks threaten the forced imposition of limits on societies in the future, while more sustainable, less consumerist lifestyles can be an expression of and contribution to freedom, now and for generations to come. Self-chosen limits set people free. If, as individuals and societies, we can choose to live within limits, a democratic transition to a more sustainable world is possible.[58]

Such lifestyle changes, guided by the norm of sufficiency, would aim to replicate, to a certain extent, what people in poverty actually do – not out of choice, but out of necessity.

Low-income households are the real experts in how to save energy, to minimize the use of water, or to lengthen the life of consumer items by sharing, reusing and repairing. Of course, these are not really 'choices': they are constrained by economic necessity. However, the experience of people in poverty presents a strong argument for improving their participation in the collective effort towards the definition of sustainable consumption at the local level, in the spirit of what the scholars working on norms of sufficiency suggest.[59] Such participation would also ensure that decisions around what should be considered as sustainable consumption take into account the specific circumstances low-income households face, thus ensuring that they are not only more effective because better informed, but also perceived as legitimate. In this area, as in many others, by failing to build on the experience of poverty, we deprive ourselves of knowledge indispensable to the search for solutions: this increases the risk not only that the measures adopted will face resistance, but also that they will be less well informed by the daily experience of these groups of the population.

The broken compass

In affluent societies, both on the left and on the right, the search for growth has turned into an obsessive quest: it is presented as the answer to the most pressing challenges societies face. Yet the obsessive search for growth has become counterproductive. Growth is bound to disappoint. And it is bound to aggravate the ecological crisis. At the same time, the quest for growth also leads to policymaking being distorted in favour of instruments that, while they may maximize efficiency gains and thus monetary value, at the same time undermine other values – and may actually end up worsening inequalities and poverty.

This can be seen in both the reliance on economic globalization as a source of growth, and, at the domestic level, in the commodification of ever more spheres of life in the never-ending search for opportunities to create value. Such strategies put efficiency above resilience, and the search for profits above the search for equality. They transform the world and people into resources to exploit. They too contribute to the counter-productivity of growth.

GLOBALIZATION: MAXIMIZING EFFICIENCY GAINS THROUGH TRADE AND INVESTMENT

Particularly since the 1980s, and even more so since the fall of the Berlin Wall and the collapse of the Soviet Union, many countries have been encouraged to open themselves up to trade and foreign investment in the name of stimulating growth. They have been advised to lower import and export tariffs, and to enter into free trade agreements. They have been told to create a 'business-friendly' environment to attract foreign investment. This, they have been told by the international financial institutions providing them with advice (and the loans that lead the advice to be taken seriously), should allow them to expand the economy and thus allow them to reimburse their debt, allowing them to access international finance.

These arguments in favour of globalization are oversold.

The assumption underlying trade liberalization is that each jurisdiction will specialize in certain lines of production that correspond to its 'comparative advantage', that is, to what it is relatively better at delivering to global markets. The idea makes intuitive sense: the deepening of the international division of labour should allow efficiency gains that all countries could potentially benefit from, since goods and services will be provided at a lower cost, and therefore be more affordable for consumers.

This reasoning, however, fails on a number of points. First, what you specialize in matters. It is not the same to specialize in the exploitation of mineral resources or in the production of raw agricultural materials, as many low-income countries have done, as it is to specialize in the production of machine tools or of manufactured goods, or in the delivery of services, which are lines of production in which opportunities for increasing value through technological advances are much higher. This is what Eduardo Galeano expressed with admirable concision in the opening words of *The Open Veins of Latin America*: 'The division of labour among nations is that some specialize in winning and others in losing.'[60] And this, of course, was at the heart of the 'structuralist approach' promoted by Raúl Prebisch, the first head, in 1948, of the Economic Commission for Latin American and the Caribbean and the first Secretary-General of the United Nations Conference on Trade and Development when it was established in 1964. Challenging forms of 'unequal trade' that exposed developing countries to deteriorating terms of trade was a major part of the quest for a 'New International Economic Order' promoted within the United Nations by these countries after they achieved political independence in the 1950s and 1960s: this agenda remains entirely valid today.[61]

Second, the deep restructuring economies go through as they seek to specialize imposes disruptions on societies that often disproportionately affect those living in poverty. In low-income countries, peasants cultivating small plots of land primarily to feed their communities are gradually marginalized, as they have been forced to compete against farmers located in rich countries who are far better equipped to achieve economies of scale and to produce large volumes of commodities, and are, moreover, often heavily subsidized by taxpayers' money; it is also these small-scale farmers, as already noted, who face the most important obstacles in entering global value chains, due to their inability to produce large volumes and to comply with the demands of large buyers, who enjoy a disproportionate bargaining power. In high-income countries, it is low-skilled workers who are the most affected. The outsourcing of production to low-wage countries has increased inequalities in rich countries, which goes a long way towards explaining such a diminution of life expectancy among certain parts of the US population, as a result of high suicide rates, drug use and alcohol consumption – what Anne Case and Angus Deaton call 'deaths of despair', especially prevalent among the white working-class population.[62] Low-skilled workers have been made to feel redundant, and increasingly desperate that their situation will not improve: scholars working on the US have highlighted that counties more exposed to the shock of trade liberalization leading to a decline in manufacturing employment exhibit higher rates of suicide and related causes of death, concentrated among white people, especially white males.[63] These trends also explain in part the success of populist parties. Such parties can easily prey upon the discontent created by the disruptions brought about by economic globalization: their preferred method of attracting voters is by invoking nostalgia for peaceful and harmonious societies undisturbed by foreign competition.

Of course, in theory, as trade leads each country to specialize, the winners should compensate the losers; the most competitive sectors, which can expand by exporting to global markets, should be taxed in order to support the compensation of workers displaced from the least competitive sectors, and their retraining. In practice, things have worked out very differently: many states have failed to provide such protection at adequate levels, and especially to ensure that the losers in this set-up are provided with meaningful and decent work.

The assumption behind investment liberalization is equally questionable. Foreign investment, according to the mainstream narrative, will benefit the local economy by accelerating technology transfers, by creating jobs, by improving access to global networks of production and distribution, and by favouring the emergence, within the state hosting the investment, of supply chains to serve the needs of the investor. Moreover, by taxing the profits made by the foreign investor, public revenue will increase.

In practice however, such linkages to the host economy are largely nullified by the very strategies countries put in place in order to favour investment. As they compete with one another to attract investors, they provide 'tax holidays', and they show a greater tolerance for transfer pricing and other schemes transnational corporations can rely on to reduce their tax liability. They rush to enter into investment treaties that bar them from imposing 'performance standards' on foreign investors, such as ensuring that they reinvest part of their profits in the local economy, that they recruit domestic workers, or contract from local suppliers. And they agree to extended protections of intellectual property rights that are obstacles to the very technology transfers they aspire to.

Such extended privileges granted to investors not only significantly diminish the benefits they bring to the host country, they also fail to actually increase the levels of investment because almost all countries end up providing a comparable standard of protection.[64] Inter-jurisdictional competition to attract investors becomes a game in which all countries end up losing: the more investors can choose to build production plants where environmental regulations are lax or under-enforced, to employ workers where wages are low and unions weak, or to declare profits where corporate income taxes are low or non-existent, the less states can, in fact, ensure that the public interest, rather than an increase in profits for shareholders, takes priority.

CREATING VALUE BY COMMODIFYING LIFE

Stimulating growth has also meant, in many cases, accelerating the commodification of life. As the economist Robert Heilbroner once noted, the expansion of capital requires that:

> daily life [be] scanned for possibilities that can be brought within the circuit of accumulation. [...] The steady movement of such tasks as laundering, cooking, cleaning, and simple health care – not to mention recreation and entertainment – from the exclusive concern of the private household into the world of business testifies to the internal expansion of capital within the interstices of social life.[65]

Heilbroner saw this commodification of life as a major source of growth in advanced economies. The long-term impacts on the sustainability of our development pathway can hardly be overstated.

We now live in a world in which rich people can pay surrogate mothers to bear their child for them; in which people in poverty are paid to be human guinea pigs to test drugs for pharmaceutical companies; in which you can buy the right to drive in fast lanes on days of busy traffic, lanes which otherwise are reserved for pooled cars; in which you can avoid standing for long hours in queues by paying someone, often a homeless or a jobless person, to wait for you; in which you can buy the right to pollute the environment, by 'offsetting' your carbon emissions as an individual, or by buying carbon credits in emissions trading (or 'cap-and-trade') schemes as companies or as countries; or in which you can pay someone to find the right partner for you or to act as your friend.[66]

What in a still recent past was provided as a service between neighbours, friends or family members, is now bought at market value from strangers. What was allocated on the basis of need, or on a first-come, first-served, basis, is now allocated on the basis of the ability to pay. What was not valued in monetary terms is now given a price tag. As the market logic expands its reach to colonize new spheres of life that go beyond the exchange of goods and services produced in order to respond to demand, the world and its people are transformed into resources to exploit, for the sake of increasing profits.

Economists rely on three arguments to defend this evolution. First, they note that reliance on economic incentives – on 'price signals' – may be the most effective way to bring about a change in the behaviour of individuals or economic actors, for the sake of moving towards greater sustainability. Provided the mix of taxes and subsidies is correct, the argument goes, such changes would be easier to achieve by putting a price tag on behaviour that has a negative impact (such as polluting) and by rewarding behaviour that instead should be encouraged (such as recycling). Thus, commodification itself is not the problem: it can in fact be an opportunity, provided the prices are right – adequately reflecting scarcity and fully internalizing externalities. Second, they consider that prohibiting certain transactions would be paternalistic, as it would violate the right of each individual to choose what he or she values the most. In other terms, putting a price tag on everything would be preferable to regulating access through other means, because individuals would remain free to choose what to do with their lives: provided they are willing to pay the price, they could even indulge in wasteful consumption or in addictive behaviour, if that is what they want. The conditions for a pluralistic society, that does not impose a moral code on its members, would therefore be preserved. Third, they argue that exchanges that are by definition mutually beneficial increase overall utility, as this makes the parties better off and leaves no one worse off. Indeed, why else would the parties to the transaction have agreed to the exchange?

In sum, the trend towards the increased commodification of life would promise a combination of efficiency and sustainability, reconciling two goals that have sometimes been presented as conflicting. The suggestions of the Chicago economist Ronald H. Coase on how to deal with the 'social cost' of economic activities (what others call externalities) are one particularly influential version of the argument in favour of commodification. In a paper published in 1960, that led to him being awarded the Nobel Prize in Economics thirty years later, Coase argued that if transaction costs are low enough (and, ideally, reduced to zero), the freedom of transactions will result in solutions that are the most economically efficient.[67] The basic reasoning is simple enough: the buyer of property will pay the price he considers reasonable, taking into consideration the streams of income are expected to flow from making a productive use of the assets acquired; therefore, if such assets are transferred to the highest bidder, as a well-functioning market for property rights should allow, they should ultimately be captured by the economic actors who can use them most productively. The 'clarification of property rights', in sum (a codeword for increased commodification), would both stimulate economic growth, and ensure that social norms or ethical concerns will not distract economic actors from the search for the most efficient use of scarce resources.

Commodification however, and the colonization of all spheres of life by market logic, come at a high cost to society.

Just like economic growth in general, it can turn out to be counter-productive.

It is not at all obvious, first of all, that rewarding people to do certain things through monetary incentives is the most effective way to promote certain types of behaviour. Financial incentives may in fact crowd out other incentives, based on norms of reciprocity or altruism. This is why, in his last book published in 1970, Richard Titmuss considered that blood donations should be made freely, rather than compensated for with a monetary reward: comparing how blood was supplied in a range of countries, but emphasizing the difference between the British system (where blood is donated for free by volunteers) and the system operating in the United States (where most of the blood is given against a payment), Titmuss noted that the latter system not only increased the risk that blood donors selling their blood would lie in order to be able to obtain the economic reward from providing blood, but also that it would not necessarily lead to a higher supply.[68] The same reasoning also explains why residents of a neighbourhood may in fact be more open to accepting a landfill site or a dumping ground for radioactive material, despite the inconvenience and risks involved, out of a sense of civic duty, than if they are offered a monetary gain as compensation: while no one wants to be seen to agree to compromising on health for profit, many might like to be seen to act out of a sense of community duty.[69] And this is also why volunteers who campaign for a good cause perform better in the absence of financial reward, than if provided with some monetary incentive.[70] People may be more motivated to do things for ethical reasons than in order to make money, and the introduction of a price mechanism may in fact corrupt the act of acting on a more altruistic basis, crowding out a sense of duty towards others.

Second, and more generally, treating certain goods or services as mere commodities devalues them. By giving them a monetary value instead of treating them as things that should be provided as a gift, or because social norms prescribe that they be provided to those who need them, these goods or services are reduced to dollars or pounds: they thus lose their singularity and their significance in social relations. For people in poverty, the commodification of social life may have other, more direct impacts. First, the more the 'commodity space' expands – the more the goods and services we need are subject to economic transactions at market value – the more income matters. For people in poverty, a world in which a large range of things required for a decent life must be paid for, and can be bought by the highest bidder, is much worse than a world in which such things are treated as 'commons', democratically governed and allocated on the basis of need, or provided by the state as part of its duty to guarantee the welfare of its population. The pursuit of commodification thus further marginalizes people in poverty. In fact, the processes of commodification and of privatization have gone so far that it can be argued that it has barely been compensated for by the expansion of the welfare state (the growing proportion of public budget that goes to alleviating poverty), spectacular as it has been since the Second World War.

Finally, while people in poverty may be attracted to the economic transactions that emerge from this commodification of the social, they will often agree to the terms proposed as a result of a form of duress, that stems from their situation of need. The reason why freedom of contract is valued in political philosophy is because of the assumption that contracts are freely negotiated between two parties, both of whom not only have full legal capacity but also are sufficiently equipped to be immune from any form of coercion. Coercion, however, may result not only from a person being literally forced to sign a contract, for instance by a gun being directed at them, but also from the *economic pressure* that may result from a party not having real alternatives, because of their weak economic position. 'Freedom' for people living on low incomes may result in coercion in that sense: when they have urgent needs to satisfy but the support provided by the state or by informal networks is so insufficient that the person cannot realistically refuse the offer that is made – even if this means selling one's kidney, providing sexual services, or standing in a line for others whose time the market values at a much higher price.[71]

In other words, we may be paying a very high price, as societies, for accepting the gradual expansion of the market logic into spheres such as intimate relationships or the fight for a clean and healthy environment, which hitherto have been governed by norms other than those of the monetary economy.

The one positive contribution of this deployment of the logic of capitalism, of course, is that many activities that were performed by women, in the form of unremunerated and unrecognized work within the household, can now be outsourced to the market. But that is a pyrrhic victory: the commodification of life may in fact have provided a convenient pretext to delay the real redistribution of gender roles and, despite their massive entry into paid employment, women continue to shoulder most of the burden of household and care responsibilities. Certain of the responsibilities traditionally assumed by women have migrated to the sphere of services provided through the market, allowing at least those women who are better off to free up time and to improve their economic independence by gaining access to paid employment outside the home. Yet, unless gender roles are effectively redistributed, women now shoulder a double or triple burden – since, in addition to waged employment, many still disproportionately assume chores within the household and caring responsibilities.

The state–market duopoly and the capture of democracy

The counter-productivity of growth is also manifest in the narrowing of democracy that results from the quest for growth. In the conventional approach to combating poverty, the need to increase monetary wealth calls for a close alliance between the state and the market, between government and the entrepreneurial class. To the extent that the state depends on economic prosperity to finance its redistributive policies and to ensure its popular legitimacy, it must ensure that markets can operate within a regulatory and economic framework that maximizes their ability to create wealth – investing in infrastructure, guaranteeing freedom of enterprise, and acting as a lender of last resort to rescue enterprises that are 'too big to fail'. This is the 'glass ceiling' facing any state looking to change the course of its development: it has become a 'state imperative' to facilitate capital accumulation and growth.[72]

Two consequences have followed. First, the state–market condominium that emerges is one that narrows down the space for the 'commons' to exist, let alone to prosper and expand. Throughout the twentieth century, this space, in which communities democratically govern certain resources or institutions, has either been privatized (with a view to maximizing profits), or bureaucratized (and coopted within the state apparatus). As a result, democratic life has been impoverished, often reduced to the ritual of elections.

While the state has been democratized, society has been de-democratized, and while citizens are asked to choose, through elections, who will make decisions on their behalf, they have also been asked to renounce deciding for themselves. The current revival of the idea of the 'commons', beyond the state–market duopoly, is a 'counter-movement'. It is a reaction against this trend. It illustrates the growing impatience with the current alliance between government and business interests.[73]

The second consequence of this alliance between the state and vested economic interests is that policymaking has been systematically skewed in favour of the most powerful corporations: private actors that have now increased their ability to distort even democratic processes. Their success has less to do with corruption or lobbying than with their ability to present themselves as the champions of economies of scale, of efficiency gains through the segmentation of the production process across jurisdictions, and of the control of worldwide logistical networks. Mass consumption requires mass production. The emptying out of democratic politics has often been the price to pay for both.

Martin Gilens and Benjamin Page have illustrated how decision making by elected representatives systematically favours large corporations – the economic elites – betraying the expectations of ordinary people.[74] And while their empirical work is focused on the situation of the United States, where money plays a particularly important role in politics,[75] this is not an exceptional case. In fact, this phenomenon has become worse with the growth of inequalities over the past forty years. A study covering 136 countries for the period 1981–2011 showed that 'as income inequality increases, rich people enjoy greater political power and respect for civil liberties than poor people do'.[76] Capture by economic elites has gone global. It was the exception; it has become the rule.[77]

In its flagship 2017 *Trade and Development Report*, the United Nations Conference for Trade and Development (UNCTAD) warns that 'increasing market concentration in leading sectors of the global economy and the growing market and lobbying powers of dominant corporations are creating a new form of global rentier capitalism to the detriment of balanced and inclusive growth for the many'.[78] The warning appears in a chapter titled 'Market power and inequality: The revenge of the rentiers', one of the most powerful indictments of the abuse by corporations of their power to influence political decision making in their favour.

The chief aim of abuses of dominant positions is to extract a rent: a 'surplus profit', representing the difference between the typical profits that should be expected and the actual profits made. This has measurable economic consequences, widening inequalities, reducing the portion of value that goes to labour and increasing the portion that goes to capital, and further worsening the imbalances in the economic system. Indeed, the share of value created going to workers has been falling consistently during the past forty years, while the share going to capital (in the form of dividends distributed to shareholders) has increased. According to a study of the International Monetary Fund, the share of labour as a percentage of GDP has been declining since the 1980s; it fell from 66.1 per cent to 61.7 per cent between 1990 and 2009 in OECD countries, reaching its lowest level before the global financial crisis of 2008, without recovering since.[79] In the United States, the decline of labour's share of income accelerated from 2000, accounting for three quarters of the decrease since 1947; 11 per cent of this decline is attributable to the impacts of globalization and automation on the reduced bargaining power of workers.[80] In advanced economies in general, the share of income going to labour is now 4 percentage points below its level of the 1970s, decreasing from 55 per cent in 1973 to 51 per cent in 2016.[81]

This evolution can be attributed to globalization – favouring the offshoring of production and strengthening the bargaining power of companies at the expense of workers – as well as to automation, but also to the sheer abuse by large corporations of their dominant economic position. UNCTAD estimates that for the top 100 firms, 40 per cent of the profits made today are the result of 'rents', a percentage that has increased from 16 per cent in the years 1995–2000 and 30 per cent in the years 2001–8. This trend is largely attributable to stronger market concentration: 10 per cent of the world's publicly listed companies capture 80 per cent of the profits. It also results from the ability of the most powerful actors to shape the competitive environment to their advantage. What emerges, UNCTAD writes, is 'a vicious cycle of under-regulation and regulatory capture, on the one hand, and further rampant growth of corporate market power on the other'.[82] The Italian-born economist Luigi Zingales refers to this as the 'vicious cycle of the Medici': money is used to influence politics, and political influence is used to make money.[83]

Economic globalization was initially promoted by states, in order to stimulate growth by expanding markets. Globalization, however, is now increasingly shaped by the international division of labour resulting from the strategies of transnational firms, strategies that states are now finding out they are hardly equipped to oppose. This imposes a major limitation on the ability of governments to promote a social and ecological transition: any measure that might reduce the profitability of investments under their jurisdictions can either be challenged as a violation of investors' rights or lead to a threat of outsourcing production, giving considerable weight to large firms in political decision making. 'Competitive' states today are states that have become powerless: obsessed with maintaining high rates of growth, governments have unilaterally disarmed themselves.

This rise in the political influence of dominant economic actors has gone hand in hand with the weakening ability of people in poverty to be heard in democratic processes. In fact, the more affluent a society becomes, the less people in poverty will have a say in how decisions are made. The reason is mathematical: the fewer they are, the less people in poverty count as a constituency politicians cannot afford to ignore. Moreover, people in poverty are less well organized, and have fewer resources than other social groups to influence decision making. They also vote less. This may explain why, as Michael Ignatieff deplored: 'Abundant societies that could actually solve the problem of poverty seem to care less about doing so than societies of scarcity that can't.'[84] The very fact that poverty has declined removes the issue from the agenda of mainstream politics, and the remaining islands of poverty appear even more difficult to address.

The capture of democracy is an obstacle, of course, for the adoption of policies that redistribute wealth and income. But it is also a problem for the transformation of societies into low-carbon societies that halt the erosion of biodiversity. As Joachim Spangenberg remarks:

> The current version of thin liberal democracy permits a certain degree of citizen influence on political decisions, but it severely restricts full participation in precisely those areas that really count from an environmental point of view such as consumption options, investment, production, and technology. Democracy tends to end at the factory entrance and a strongly sustainable society will need to change that, strengthening and extending the democratic domain.[85]

Democracy should be deepened in two directions: direct participation, in particular of people in poverty, should be encouraged; and the democratic requirement should extend to new areas, particularly firms, from where it has, until now, been excluded (I return to this point later). Indeed, only by such a deepening of democracy will it be possible to move to more sustainable lifestyles in ways that will be perceived as legitimate and the result of self-determination. This will be more effective than where such lifestyle changes are imposed by technocratic fiats or through the use of economic incentives, however 'smart' such incentives may be.

3

The Strange Persistence of the Ideology of Growth

Economic growth, then, as measured by increases in GDP, is unable to deliver on its promises. It barely contributes to the improvement of well-being. It is hardly reconcilable with sustainability objectives. And it skews policy and decision making in favour of economic elites. How, then, can we explain its persistent hold on the imagination of policymakers? Why is it adhered to as strongly as if it has become a new secular faith, more powerful even than the religious faiths of the past? At least three explanations emerge.

Creating jobs and investing in development

The first reason has already been noted: while growth cannot be endorsed as a universal prescription, and certainly should not guide policies in the global North, it is still a meaningful objective for lower-income countries. In part, this is because of demographic growth. An additional 470 million people will be looking for work in developing countries between 2019 and 2035,[1] with a particularly fast growth in sub-Saharan Africa.[2]

The hope, then, is that growth will create more jobs. It should be immediately added, however, that some forms of growth, such as those that are based on the exploitation of natural resources[3] or on labour-saving technological advances,[4] can disappoint such expectations: not all growth is job-rich, and if growth is to deliver on the promise of job creation, it should go hand in hand with policies that deliberately aim at full employment.[5]

Another reason why the search for growth remains meaningful in low-income countries, of course, is because infrastructures remain insufficient, and because a number of essential needs are still not met: growth therefore remains closely correlated to the improvement of well-being, as it can allow schools and hospitals to be built, wells to be dug and irrigation schemes set up, or communication networks to be upgraded for the benefit of the population. Yet, here again, it is not growth as such that will suffice: growth will only be useful if it allows public revenue to increase, and if that revenue in turn is spent to meet the needs of the population. Growth can be a tool for development. But if its benefits are pocketed by a narrow economic elite, or captured by transnational corporations that will send their profits to low-tax jurisdictions or to tax havens, or if the government revenue is not invested for the people, the recipe will fail.

Ensuring the public debt is sustainable

The second reason is that almost all countries face high levels of public debt. This is true, of course, of developing countries. By the spring of 2023, 60 per cent of low-income countries were either in or at high risk of debt distress, and many middle-income countries were also facing increasing debt vulnerabilities. Squeezed by rising interest rates and by currency depreciation (some ninety developing countries have seen their currencies weakened against the dollar in 2022 – over a third of them by more than 10 per cent), a number of countries have already defaulted on their debt, or are undergoing debt restructuring.

The debt of developing countries, and of low-income countries in particular, limits the ability of these countries to provide basic services to their population and to strengthen social protection. The challenge is not limited to developing countries, however. Advanced economies too face high levels of public debt, and they too must borrow on financial markets in order to fund the services they provide to the population. While the OECD average debt-to-GDP ratio was 89 per cent in 2022, the total figure (for all OECD countries combined) was 121 per cent, and some countries were significantly above the average: the figures were 192 per cent for Greece, 173 per cent for Italy, 144 per cent for the United States and 104 per cent for the United Kingdom.[6] Since the debt would be even more expensive to pay back if the economy were to stagnate or, even worse, were to fall into a recession, such high levels of public debt provide a strong argument in favour of growth; indeed, it would seem obvious enough that the re-igniting of growth is the condition for any poverty-reduction policy, whatever precise form it takes.

The argument, however, underestimates the large panoply of tools that states have to maintain public debt within acceptable limits – acceptable, that is, to the creditors from whom they need to borrow during economic downturns. More could be done to fight against aggressive tax optimization strategies by transnational firms – including through improved international cooperation to reduce tax competition – and to combat tax evasion. New welfare-enhancing taxes could be introduced, such as a tax on unhealthy foods or on fuel-thirsty SUVs.

Equally, considerable revenues could be collected by introducing or raising wealth taxes or inheritance taxes where they are low or even non-existent. Indeed, wealth concentration is today, even more so than in the past, largely the result of intergenerational transfers such as inheritance and gifts.[7]

The share of inherited wealth has grown in Europe and the United States from 30–40 per cent during the period 1950–80 to 50–60 per cent since 2010.[8] This reinforces the intergenerational perpetuation of poverty, since the likelihood of receiving an inheritance or gift increases with wealth rank.[9] Increasing taxes on inheritance would therefore be a coherent way of tackling wealth inequalities. Yet only 24 out of 37 OECD countries tax inheritance, estates or gifts across generations and, even where they exist, the levies are typically very low, accounting for only 0.5 per cent of total tax revenues on average for the 24 countries concerned.[10]

In an ideal world, the prescription would be simple: governments faced with high levels of debt should seek to finance themselves (both to reimburse the debt and to continue to provide public services to the population) by taxing the 'ills' more (such as the exploitation of fossil energies or the consumption of luxury items), while at the same time reducing taxes on the 'goods' (such as labour). Growing the economy, in other terms, is not the only way to address the debt issue: another possibility is to increase public revenue from whatever wealth or activities already exist, thus at the same time reducing wealth disparities and discouraging certain activities that are toxic, producing high negative externalities.

This, however, is not an ideal world. It is a world in which even the best-intended solutions can meet with resistance, and in which the schemes that look the neatest on paper may stumble on the reality of poor people's lives.

Consider, for example, the much-debated question of whether a carbon tax should be introduced. In theory, a carbon tax is a tool both to increase public revenue and to encourage the changes needed in investment, production, and consumption patterns – a means of supporting technological innovations that can decrease future abatement costs: it is typically what we call a 'win-win'.

Indeed, the experiences of Sweden, or of the Canadian provinces of British Columbia and of Alberta, illustrate that carbon taxes are not only a means to accelerate the ecological transformation, and to increase state revenues: they can also contribute to poverty reduction, provided the revenues raised are used to support low-income households.[11] In 1991 Sweden became one of the first jurisdictions to establish a carbon tax, and today it has the highest carbon tax in the world (at US$127 per ton of CO_2 in 2019). The carbon tax led to a significant fall of carbon intensity of the economy, leading some scholars to argue that Sweden provides a rare example of an absolute decoupling of growth from emissions: while the economy grew by 69 per cent in the period 1990–2015, they argue, emissions declined by 26 per cent over the same period.[12] Commentators attribute this success story to the fact that environmental taxation coincided with the lowering of corporate and labour taxes, so that the implementation of a carbon tax was perceived as an opportunity to transfer taxation to 'bad goods' rather than taxing labour or non-polluting inputs.[13] In the Canadian province of Alberta, the revenues from the carbon-pricing mechanisms (including both an ETS [emissions trading system] and a carbon tax) served to finance mitigation and adaptation projects, but also to provide for tax rebates to low- and middle-income households, covering in total 60 per cent of households: in 2019 the rebate was set at US$337 for the first adult, US$169 for the second adult, and US$51 for each child, while low-income individuals or families were guaranteed a full rebate.[14] The carbon tax introduced in British Columbia enjoyed broad political support (with opposition to carbon pricing decreasing in the population from 60 per cent to less than 45 per cent between 2009 and 2015),[15] in particular because, as in Sweden, the carbon price was raised gradually, and because it was combined with tax credits for households to protect affordability (US$152 per adult and

US$45 per child for 2018).[16] Comparative studies thus show that, provided communities are involved in shaping the solutions, and provided communication is transparent about the use of the revenues from carbon taxes and the outcome is perceived as fair, the carbon tax can be socially acceptable and can be seen as a tool of social progress.[17]

In reality, things are not that simple. In order to introduce a carbon tax, political economy considerations should first be borne in mind. Whereas benefits from reduced greenhouse gas emissions are diffused and spread over the mid-term and long-term, costs imposed by explicit carbon pricing – as well as the costs of implicit carbon pricing, such as levying taxes or reducing subsidies on fossil fuels – are concentrated on certain actors and are felt in the short term.[18] In fact, this is a case in which both powerful economic actors associated with the most polluting industries (in particular the extractive industry) and anti-poverty groups could form a paradoxical alliance in defence of the status quo: a carbon tax would reduce the profitability of those industries at the same time as it would increase the cost of energy for low-income households. Opposition could therefore come from both groups, despite them otherwise having so little in common. Second, in practice, many measures designed to 'compensate' low-income earners for the increased costs of energy resulting from the introduction of a carbon tax could never reach them: many studies have highlighted the issue of 'non-take-up' of benefits by disadvantaged households who, for a variety of reasons (ranging from a lack of information to the complexity of administrative procedures and the specific obstacles people face when having to claim certain benefits through online applications), may not in fact be able to access certain benefits ostensibly designed to help them.[19]

Therefore, while the carbon tax is highly desirable in theory, and can be a tool both to accelerate the change in production and consumption and to combat poverty, it can only be implemented in a context in which the government is trusted by the people, and in which specific attention is given to the concrete obstacles low-income households face in seeking support. Unless these conditions are met, it will spark resistance.

Buying social peace

There is a third and perhaps even more immediate reason why economic growth continues to provide the compass for public policy: it is political expediency. Growth has the unique virtue of bridging views from across both the left and the right. Progressive politicians can accept renouncing the radical vision of redistribution on a large scale against the promise of a steady improvement of the living conditions of low-income groups made possible thanks to growth; if the size of the pie expands and if part of that expansion benefits those groups, it should matter less if the slices going to them are much smaller than those going to the wealthiest parts of society. Conservatives will easily concur. They see growth as a justification for pursuing the pro-business policies their supporters expect from them, and they too are ready to compromise: they see sharing the benefits of growth as a substitute for broader social transformations based on redistribution that would threaten the vested economic interests on which they depend.

Growth, therefore, appears consensual: the median voter will be in favour of it, and it is convenient for politicians to promise it. How to achieve it and what should be done with it may be more contentious: Will it be achieved by liberalizing trade and by intensifying work, or by supporting the purchasing power of the poorest groups of society? Will it be captured by a handful of bold entrepreneurs, or will it be widely redistributed? Those questions will divide opinion. But growth at least seems desirable to all; no wonder it remains the lodestar, despite all the problems associated with our endless pursuit of it.

* * *

Something else is needed. Modern poverty will persist as long as we continue to allow inequalities of wealth and income to blur the distinction between needs and desires. And we will continue to erode the natural capital on which all human activity ultimately depends, both as a provider of resources and as a sink to absorb our waste,[20] if we continue to insist on economic growth as the solution to society's ills.

Yet alternatives to this dominant model of development have been systematically sidelined. 'Zero-growth' approaches to environmental sustainability[21] have been marginalized or entirely ignored.[22] We have been taught to believe that there is an inevitable tension between poverty reduction and ecological sustainability. Such a tension persists, however, only because of a lack of political imagination, and because of a conception of the fight against poverty that depends on increasing wealth.

We must escape this straitjacket. Alternative development pathways should urgently be sketched. It is time to move beyond the idea that economic growth is a precondition for a convivial and sustainable society.

4

The Post-growth Approach to Combating Poverty

Growth remains necessary in low-income countries. Even in those countries, however, its poverty-reducing impact will only be felt if it primarily benefits the most disadvantaged groups of society: where it goes hand in hand with a growth in inequalities, it will not serve the purpose of human development.[1]

Growth that is fuelled by the exploitation of natural resources presents particular challenges in this regard. Residents of resource-rich countries may suffer from weak governance and impoverishment not despite but rather *because of* their abundant and widely coveted natural wealth, and the efforts to exploit such resources. This is not only because the exploitation of mineral resources should be seen as the consumption of capital rather than a stream of income (and agriculture, when it is practised in a way that is not sustainable, presents a striking similarity to mining). It is also because the exploitation of natural resources typically takes the form of large-scale projects in which a small number of individuals control vast amounts of wealth. The capture and distribution of benefits can therefore be highly unequal unless affirmative measures are taken to ensure that benefits will be fairly allocated across all those who are affected. The temptation is also huge for those in power at the government and corporate levels to exploit these resources in order to create as much wealth as possible within the shortest possible time (since these individuals do not know how long they will stay in power) and to sell off the right to exploit these resources to the highest bidder (in order to cash in immediately on the equivalent of all future income streams that could result from exploiting the resource). GDP growth, when combined with such a 'resource curse' (as this phenomenon has come to be known among political scientists),[2] is counter-productive.

Rich countries face their own challenges in steering development in the right direction, and it is these countries on which I focus here. In these countries, more political imagination is required in order to move beyond growth: can the fight against poverty and environmental sustainability be achieved without relying on the increase of monetary wealth – in what Herman Daly called a 'steady-state economy'?[3] I believe the equation can be solved, by combining a range of instruments, and by coordinating change across different sectors.

Not all these instruments can be explored here. In particular, which techniques we have designed and have been encouraged to use would deserve separate treatment.[4] To a large extent, technological development has been driven by the quest for innovations that could increase efficiency (the output produced per input invested in production), in order to raise profits for the benefit of economic actors controlling the production process. As the main 'social carriers' of techniques have been for-profit companies,[5] particular emphasis was placed on technological innovations that could save labour: by improving labour productivity, it was anticipated, wages would be allowed to increase, and a higher purchasing power would result in improved well-being. As we already noted, however, this meant that whereas growth was intended to create jobs, its bias towards labour-saving techniques not unusually led growth to go hand in hand with jobs being destroyed: indeed, jobless growth has become routine since the

1970s. Whatever jobs were created as a result of technological innovations, moreover, were generally far more resource- and energy-intensive. And work has not been eased, it has rather been intensified: the very technologies that were deployed to favour productivity gains have also resulted in workers relating to the technologies as a dog relates to his master – serving them, obeying them, aligning with their temporalities, and often depriving workers of the very autonomy and creativity that can make work truly rewarding.

The broader problem is that technological development has often taken on a life of its own, responding to a logic based on the maximization of shareholder value, rather than being guided by broader societal values. These were the concerns already expressed two generations ago by Ernst Schumacher or, in the French-speaking world, by Jacques Ellul.[6] In the process of innovation, high-tech took priority above low-tech, leading to the tools we use being less 'convivial', understandable and controllable by the user;[7] rapid obsolescence for consumer items was favoured above the production of items easy to repair and reuse, and with a longer use-life; automation served to concentrate power and increase control rather than to encourage collaboration and care as 'post-automation' might;[8] technological innovations, finally, were prioritized above social innovations.

This last hierarchy is particularly illustrative of our failure to put innovation in service of a post-growth society – a society that chooses well-being, not growth, as its priority.[9] Unlike technological innovations, social innovations cannot be fenced by intellectual property rights, and they are not handed over from scientists and engineers working in large firms to users. Instead, they are democratic. They are shared in open access. They are grown organically and bottom-up. They do not lead to centralization but to decentralization. They do not lead to the dissemination of uniform solutions, demanding from people that they adapt to technologies that are imposed on them in the name of 'progress'; instead, social innovations promote and value diversity, the result of the search by local communities for the solutions that are best suited to the particular contexts in which they live. They do not disempower, and they do not result in new dependencies: they are empowering and promote autonomy and self-determination.[10] Yet, all these reasons why we should value social innovations more – why we should support communities coming up with their own solutions and build on their inventiveness – are precisely the reasons why, as we fetishize growth measured through the lens of GDP, we tend to neglect them: the value created by social innovations cannot easily be monetized, and such innovations do not sufficiently serve the new divinity of growth.

A more reflective or discerning attitude towards technological pathways and innovation in general should therefore be included among the instruments that can lead us towards a post-growth society. Here, however, I emphasize three other avenues. Their common characteristic is that they are particularly well suited to reconcile the ecological transformation with the social transformation.

First, efforts should shift towards measures that have a 'triple dividend': measures that (1) reduce the environmental impact of production and consumption, while at the same time (2) creating employment opportunities for people with lower levels of qualification, and (3) making the goods and services necessary for a life in dignity affordable for low-income households. Such measures can be identified in a range of areas, including in the key areas of energy, mobility, food and agriculture, and the building industry. A focus on such 'triple-dividend' measures would ensure that the urgent ecological transformation required can contribute to social justice.

Second, income and wealth inequalities should be combated. This is essential since, even if all households could be protected from 'severe material deprivation' (in other terms, had access to the full range of goods and services that allow a decent standard of living), social exclusion could persist due to the 'modernization' of poverty: these households still could experience exclusion if they were unable to cope with the general increase of the levels of consumption and the social expectations that follow. In other terms, reducing 'absolute' poverty by guaranteeing access to a minimum basket of goods and services necessary to satisfy basic needs would not suffice, if we continue to tolerate high levels of inequality that result in social exclusion.

Finally, the world of work should be reimagined. By guaranteeing the right to work, by democratizing work, and by reducing working hours and thus the centrality of work in people's lives, we can put employment in the service of the social and ecological transformation we so urgently need.

These are the ingredients of a convivial and sustainable society: a society that excludes no one, that ensures the well-being of all, while also maintaining consumption patterns within acceptable boundaries by encouraging a norm of sufficiency.

Triple-dividend measures

The ecological transformation of societies and poverty eradication are often seen as conflicting objectives or, at best, as objectives that compete against one another. This framing is understandable. Significant investments will be required to develop renewable energy sources or public transportation networks, or to insulate buildings, thus reducing the budgets available for the financing of public services of health or education or for social protection. In addition, the ecological transformation has typically been driven by the adoption of socially regressive measures: the introduction of 'carbon taxes' without compensatory measures for low-income households or the creation of 'low emission zones' in city centres, which amounts to a de facto exclusion of drivers who cannot afford a less polluting vehicle, have come to symbolize an approach sometimes denounced as 'punitive' and perceived as hostile to the more deprived socio-economic groups, as well as ill-informed about their lived experiences.

Yet another route exists: it is to see the ecological transformation as a lever for social justice. Indeed, there are important, yet often overlooked, synergies between the aims of ecological transformation and of poverty eradication. New employment opportunities arise from the ecological transition in key sectors of the economy,[11] and policies can be put in place to ensure that the most sustainable consumption choices are also the easiest and the most affordable.

ENERGY

In the energy sector, measures to improve energy efficiency have important job-creation potential.[12] So does the shift from fossil fuels to renewable sources of energy. Between 2012 and 2016, the number of people directly and indirectly employed in the renewable energy sector (excluding large hydropower) rose from 5.7 million to 8.3 million,[13] a figure that could increase to 25 million by 2030 with proper policy support. This would offset the job destruction in carbon-intensive industries, since renewable energy is more labour-intensive than fossil-based energy.[14] Per dollar of expenditure, spending on renewable energy will produce nearly 70 per cent more jobs than spending on fossil fuels.[15] Employment in the renewable energy industry is also of better quality than that in the fossil fuel industry,[16] and women are better represented.[17]

The transition to renewables can be designed both to support poverty eradication and to combat social exclusion.

Training programmes could target low-skilled workers in particular, or skilled workers from industries that experience job losses resulting from the energy transition.[18] Long-term commitments by states to electrify transport and heating systems, combining taxes and subsidies to favour the switch, could make access to such systems affordable for low-income households, as illustrated by the successful penetration of electrical vehicles in Norway.[19] The greening of energy can also lead to additional income for rural households, as in the case of 'solar double cropping',[20] where solar panels are spaced out and placed at a height allowing the land underneath to be used for agricultural purposes while also reducing irrigation needs.[21]

Efforts to move towards sustainable energy provision could therefore go hand in hand with efforts to ensure universal access to affordable, reliable and modern energy services, in accordance with target 7.1 of the SDGs. A large number of households still do not have access to affordable modern energy services, especially in rural communities.[22] Today, 733 million people do not have access to electricity (in comparison with 1.2 billion in 2010),[23] and 2.4 billion people still lack access to clean-cooking solutions and are exposed to dangerous levels of air pollution, causing millions of deaths each year, mostly among women and children.[24] More than one in two people in sub-Saharan Africa still lack access to electricity.

Far from the affordability of energy being in tension with the gradual substitution of fossil energies by renewable energy sources, the shift to a decarbonized energy system can accelerate progress towards universal access to energy. All 34 OECD countries have seen a positive impact of an increased share of renewable energy on the retail price of electricity.[25] The price of electricity from renewable sources is now dropping due to the decrease in production costs of solar photovoltaic and wind power technologies, as well as the economies of scale achieved.[26] Measures to promote energy efficiency can reduce energy bills for people facing poverty, thereby decreasing both the environmental footprint of households and energy poverty. Moreover, social tariff schemes – ensuring that the households that consume the least energy pay the least per kW consumed, or even that a minimum amount of energy per person is guaranteed free of charge – can offset any short-term price impacts of the switch to renewables and protect low-income households from excessive price volatility and energy poverty.

BUILDINGS

The same is true for the building sector. One billion people still live in slums[27] and ensuring access to housing should be a top priority. This should go hand in hand with improving the energy performance of buildings by ensuring dwellings are well-insulated and energy-efficient. The built environment accounts for 40 per cent of global energy use and 30 per cent of energy-related greenhouse gas emissions.[28] The potential for energy savings is therefore enormous,[29] given the low energy performance of existing buildings and the speed of urbanization in developing countries. With the right policies and technologies, energy consumption in both new and existing buildings could be cut by 30 to 80 per cent.[30]

This transformation of the construction sector would not only reduce energy bills for low-income households but also provide new jobs for people in poverty. Approximately 111 million people – or 7 per cent of the global workforce – work in the construction sector,[31] and three quarters are in developing countries, where residential construction employs up to 10 per cent of the total labour force.[32] For low-skilled workers, there are real opportunities in the retrofitting of buildings, as well as in the building of affordable housing.[33] Climate mitigation policies should increase employment by 1.7 per cent in the construction industry worldwide.[34] Every US$1 million invested in the construction sector creates close to 650 jobs in India, 200 in China, 160 in Brazil and in Indonesia, and 120 in the Russian Federation.[35]

FOOD AND AGRICULTURE

In the agrifood sector also, 'triple-dividend' measures can be identified that create jobs, ensure access to nutritious and healthy diets and reduce the environmental impacts of food production. What is required here, however, is to break vicious cycles, in an area in which path dependencies are particularly strong.

In today's dominant approach, industrial farming combines reliance on pesticides and chemical fertilizers with mechanization of production, large-scale irrigation, and the use of 'improved' plant varieties designed to increase yields. This leads to soil depletion and a loss of agrobiodiversity, and thus to a decline of soil fertility. The response has been more external inputs, and the use of heavier machinery, to maintain or even increase yields per hectare. We seem to be caught in a trap.

This technological revolution in food production started in North America and Europe in the 1920s. It later spread to Central and Latin America in the 1940s and 1950s, and then to South Asia, starting with India and Pakistan, in the mid-1960s. At the time, in the 1950s and 1960s, the spread of 'modern' farming techniques (in which the US scientist Norman Borlaug played a major role)[36] was seen as a way to prevent large-scale famines. Governments were presented with doomsday scenarios in a context of unprecedented demographic growth: as a result of higher life expectancy and reduced child and maternal mortality, the rate at which population increases reached its peak in the 1960s, with an estimated 2.19 per cent annual increase in 1963 – almost double what it is today.[37] Indeed, echoing the fears of the time, Paul R. Ehrlich and his wife Ann Howland (though she was not credited as co-author) had predicted in their 1968 best-selling book, *The Population Bomb*, that under a business-as-usual scenario, entire regions would be facing starvation because agricultural output would be unable to catch up with demographic growth and the shifting diets linked to urbanization.[38]

At the time, what came to be called the 'Green Revolution' seemed to provide a response. The mechanization of production, the development of global supply chains, and economies of scale resulted in an increase of both the volumes of agricultural commodities produced and traded, and of the supply of processed foods. In most world regions, this meant more diversified diets for the wealthiest parts of the population.

The costs to the environment and to public health have been enormous, however, and people in poverty have generally not benefited from these advances. The Intergovernmental Science-Policy Platform on Biodiversity and Ecosystem Services (IPBES) warned in 2019 that '[w]hile the value of agricultural crop production [...] has increased approximately threefold since 1970 [...] indicators of regulating contributions, such as soil organic carbon and pollinator diversity, have declined, indicating that gains in material contributions are often not sustainable'.[39] Almost one quarter of the world's land area is degraded, reducing productivity, and pollinator loss costs between US$235 billion and US$577 billion in reduced crop output.[40] While farming itself contributes around 10–12 per cent of greenhouse gas emissions (mainly from CH_4 and N_2O emissions),[41] agriculture-driven deforestation adds a further 6–17 per cent, and the food system as a whole contributes between 15 and 28 per cent to overall greenhouse gas emissions in developed countries, taking into account all stages in the supply chain, from agricultural production through to processing, distribution, retail, food preparation and waste.[42] We managed to feed the world, but at a huge cost to the ecosystems and to future generations.[43]

And the benefits were unequally spread – so much so, in fact, that peasant families in low-income countries are today the main victims of hunger. Poor rural households in many developing countries, who practise farming on a small scale, have been the most significantly affected by the pressures on land and on farmers' incomes that resulted from the Green Revolution. While competition for land and the costs of farming have increased, farm-gate prices have generally declined, squeezing out of farming, or relegating to subsistence farming, the least competitive and the most land-poor farming households. And at the consumer end of the food chain, low-income families are disproportionately affected by obesity and by the non-communicable diseases linked to the increased consumption of heavily processed foods and to the lack of dietary diversity associated with industrial food systems.[44] This is one source of the intergenerational transmission of poverty in these countries, since children born from women with obesity are at greater risk of obesity and thus of discrimination in access to employment.[45]

This too is an area in which transformative change is required, and in which triple dividends can be achieved. Low-input farming following the principles of agroecology – mimicking nature rather than industrializing farming – has a huge but still largely untapped potential to mitigate climate change: techniques such as mixed cropping schemes using leguminous plants to fertilize soils or managing pests by biological control reduce the dependency of food production on fossil energy and cut the emissions of nitrous oxide, while at the same time allowing soils to function as carbon sinks.[46] Recent reports from IPBES,[47] the Intergovernmental Panel of Experts on Climate Change (IPCC),[48] the Independent Group of Scientists appointed by the Secretary-General on the progress towards the SDGs,[49] the Global Commission on Adaptation,[50] the International Panel of Experts on Sustainable Food Systems (IPES-Food)[51] and the Committee of World Food Security's High-Level Panel of Experts on Food Security and Nutrition (HLPE)[52] have all highlighted these benefits.

More sustainable agricultural practices also reduce the costs of farming, thus benefiting rural households who practise small-scale farming in low-income countries. Because they are relatively labour-intensive, they contribute to employment creation in rural areas. They also improve the resilience of farming systems against weather-related events, including those linked to climate change. Finally, they provide adequate nutrition to local communities through the provision of diversified, safe and balanced diets.

MOBILITY

Mobility is the fourth area in which triple-dividend measures can be adopted. Transport represents between 20 and 30 per cent of the environmental impact linked to household consumption, and this impact is growing.[53] Indeed, the expected growth in the demand for passenger transport is such, that even taking into account technological improvements such as more efficient cars, worldwide transport CO_2 emissions are expected to grow by 60 per cent by 2050.[54]

Motorized transport in particular, which is still heavily reliant on fossil fuels, is a major source of CO_2 emissions,[55] and it has severe health consequences through air pollution and traffic congestion.[56] The main victims, people in low-income neighbourhoods, are the least to blame. This is a typical example of climate injustice. While underprivileged households suffer the most from the impacts of traffic pollution,[57] they contribute to the problem less than better-off households: although relatively poor households often live at a distance from work and in locations poorly connected by public transportation services, obliging them to travel in private vehicles to work,[58] the distance one travels generally increases with disposable income,[59] whether we consider the distance travelled by plane[60] or by car,[61] (respectively the first and second most greenhouse gas-emitting modes of transport).[62]

Territorial planning and public transport are two priority triple-dividend actions in the mobility sector. Territorial planning can shorten the distance between the home and places of employment and education, thus reducing the need for motorized transport and preventing the spatial segregation of the socially disadvantaged.[63] The promotion of collective modes of transport, a mix of public transport and shared mobility, combined with restricting access or prohibiting cars in dense urban areas when collective transport can cater for the needs[64] – a measure that appears fairer than congestion charges[65] – can both reduce reliance on individual vehicles and ensure a right to mobility for all.

Many hopes are currently placed on electric vehicles. Indeed, battery electric cars emit less greenhouse gas emissions over their lifetime than cars with an internal combustion engine using gasoline,[66] and the electric powering of vehicles can be a last resort solution, at least where electricity provision can be sourced from renewable sources and where strict environmental safeguards apply to battery production.[67] However, because they are so costly, electric vehicles are not a solution for people in poverty, at least for the foreseeable future. There is, moreover, a risk that the promotion of electric vehicles will perpetuate car-centric mobility at the expense of public transport and additional urban green spaces, disproportionately affecting the livelihoods and well-being of those living in poverty.[68]

In addition to improving access to services for people in poverty, often relegated to neighbourhoods far from the better-connected urban centres, investing in territorial planning and in public transport can be an important source of green job creation. Doubling investments in public transport is estimated to generate a net gain of at least 2.5 million jobs worldwide, and at least 5 million jobs when considering the broader impact on other sectors of the economy.[69] While the automobile industry will face job losses, new jobs will be created in public transportation services and in the manufacturing of the required infrastructure. Additionally, due to the cheaper cost of collective transport, the disposable income of households will increase, freeing up resources that could be spent elsewhere and leading to job creation in other sectors.

* * *

These sector-specific measures could go a long way towards establishing the conditions for a convivial and sustainable society – one that reconciles poverty eradication with the need to remain within planetary boundaries by creating jobs and ensuring that basic goods and services are more affordable for low-income households while at the same time reducing the pressures on the environment. Such measures will remain insufficient, however, unless more structural changes take place. To combat modern poverty, we must also reduce the gap between rich and poor, and move away from a work-centred society that traps us in a vicious cycle of work and consumption.

Combating inequality

There are three reasons why the fight against inequalities should now take priority. First, once we move beyond the weak definition of poverty based solely on the inability to satisfy basic needs and see it rather as the social exclusion that people face when they are unable to match the changing social expectations that result from the general increase in affluence, inequality results in poverty. Second, inequality is a major obstacle to ecological transformation as it favours unsustainable lifestyles and status competition. Third and finally, inequality pits the frivolous desires of the rich against the essential needs of people with lower incomes: it therefore leads to a deeply inefficient use of scarce resources. For all these reasons, economic growth cannot continue to serve as a substitute for a more equitable sharing of incomes and the redistribution of wealth.

INEQUALITY BREEDS POVERTY

The first and most obvious reason for seeking to combat inequalities is that, by definition, inequality perpetuates poverty.

As noted, in affluent societies poverty should be seen as a relative concept, reflecting not the absolute deprivation of the individual or household, but the position of the individual or the household within society. People are poor, according to the modern definition of poverty, if they are unable to meet social expectations because of the gap between their position and that of other members of society with whom they are compared.

In addition, more inequality means less social mobility. In more unequal societies, the lowest-income earners may find it difficult to invest in training or in education for their children (or, to speak the argot of the times, in what the Chicago economist Gary Becker labelled 'human capital').[70] Success in life depends on access to resources, both monetary and non-monetary, that rich segments of society find it easier to mobilize. Countries with greater inequality therefore tend to be countries where economic advantage and disadvantage is passed on to children. Alan Krueger, chair of the Council of Economic Advisers under President Barack Obama, described this relationship between income inequality and intergenerational income mobility as the 'Great Gatsby Curve', although the reference is rather odd: what study after study has shown is that the character in the novel of F. Scott Fitzgerald who makes it from being a bootlegger to joining the New York elite represents a rare exception to the rule.[71]

INEQUALITY IS AN OBSTACLE TO ENVIRONMENTAL SUSTAINABILITY

The fight against inequality should also be seen as an essential instrument in the ecological transformation of societies.[72] The link is obvious once we consider that the more equally the creation of wealth is spread across the population, the easier it is to reconcile ecological and poverty-reduction objectives. If the benefits of increased prosperity trickle down to the worst-off in society, less growth will be required for the basic needs of all to be met. And since growing the economy cannot be done without increasing the use of resources and the production of waste, it is imperative that, where the economy must still grow – in low-income countries, for example, where poverty reduction depends on the further creation of wealth – it does so in ways that will maximize its positive impacts on lifting people out of poverty while minimizing its ecological impacts.

Moreover, inequality stimulates status competition and thus material consumption. We 'want' material things, for the most part, not because of the comfort they provide, but for the message we send to those around us. This was a key insight of Thorstein Veblen in his *Theory of the Leisure Class*: 'the standard of expenditure which commonly guides our efforts', he wrote more than a century ago, 'is not the average, ordinary expenditure already achieved; it is an ideal of consumption that lies just beyond our reach, or to reach which requires some strain. The motive is emulation – the stimulus of an invidious comparison which prompts us to outdo those with whom we are in the habit of classing ourselves'.[73] Since 'each class envies and emulates the class next above it in the social scale, while it rarely compares itself with those below or with those who are considerably in advance',[74] unequal societies lead to a permanent race for status through consumption.[75] By contrast, in more equal societies, or in societies in which social positioning can be signalled by means other than consumption, the growth needed to feed the work-spend-consume cycle becomes less necessary.[76]

Because it reduces the pressure of social comparison, the pursuit of greater equality would thus translate into an increase in well-being, which the pursuit of economic growth alone has become unable to provide. It would also mean putting a brake on the most unsustainable lifestyles, that only the richest segments of the population can afford. In all regions, the environmental impacts of the most affluent parts of the population are significantly higher than those of low-income groups. In France for instance, taking into account not only direct energy consumption (in electricity, gas and fuel), but also the material goods consumed, the total energy consumption of the wealthiest 20 per cent of households is 2.5 times higher than the total energy consumption of the poorest 20 per cent of households.[77] Other studies estimate that the emissions of the lowest quintile of the French population are on average one third those of the highest quintile.[78]

These unsustainable lifestyles, driven by status competition and conspicuous consumption, fuel the consumption-driven model of our current global economic system, which relies on the ever-increasing production and purchase of consumer goods to sustain economic growth.

Such consumption patterns are at the heart of the 'throwaway culture' so central to today's consumption society. The practice of planning or 'building in' obsolescence – manufacturers' profit-motivated practice of deliberately designing products to fail prematurely or become out-of-date, so as to sell another product or an upgrade thereof – has become the symbol of such a culture. Rather than encouraging the repair and the reuse of consumer items, some actors prefer to deliberately shorten their lifetime – and the phenomenon is getting worse: the proportion of large household appliances that were replaced within less than five years due to the presence of a defect increased from 3.5 per cent to 8.3 per cent between 2004 and 2013, leading to higher volumes of waste and to increased resource use and greenhouse gas emissions.[79]

Again, people in poverty lose. The limited disposable income available at the time of the purchase of a consumer item may make it difficult for poor consumers to buy long-life products, which are generally more expensive but have a lower annual total cost.[80] This is a penalty imposed on low-income households: the poorer you are, the more you pay. Moreover, people in poverty are disproportionately affected by the dumping of avoidable waste, particularly from electronic products. Only 20 per cent of the total volume of global e-waste is recycled. The remainder is traded or deposited in dump sites,[81] causing environmental pollution and health hazards for the most marginalized populations, a major source of environmental injustice domestically and globally:[82] 80 per cent of electrical and electronic waste is sent to China and several African countries.[83]

The fight against premature obsolescence should therefore be made a priority to escape from the current economic system that is based on waste and ever higher levels of consumption. This may lead to employment losses in waste management and recycling, primarily in the global South.[84] Yet the net employment impacts are positive, since the repair, maintenance and rental industries have considerable job-creation potential.[85] Globally, moving away from the model of 'extract, make, use and dispose' would lead to the creation of 6 million additional jobs by 2030, a 0.1 per cent increase in employment by 2030 in comparison with a business-as-usual scenario.[86]

INEQUALITY LEADS TO INEFFICIENCY

Finally, the use of resources is more efficient in more equal societies.

Markets don't respond to needs. What they register is *demand*, as expressed in the purchasing power of consumers, in proportion of their ability to pay. Scitovsky therefore compared the marketplace to a plutocracy: it is 'the rule of the rich', he wrote, 'where each consumer's influence on what gets produced depends on how much he spends'.[87] Yet once you get to vote on the allocation of resources in proportion to the money you can put on the table, it is our sense of priorities that gets distorted. In unequal societies, the 'desires' of the most affluent may take precedence over the satisfaction of basic needs linked to housing, health, education or access to green areas for the least affluent. Greater equality mitigates this distortion.

Designing pro-poor policies and combating inequality can therefore serve to mitigate the tension between ecological sustainability and poverty reduction, and ensure that whatever economic growth there is will effectively improve the situation of people in poverty, rather than fuel consumption by the rich.

What is true at the domestic level, is even more so at the global level. Global inequalities are significantly higher than inequalities within countries. This is a major source of injustice: whether you are rich or poor today depends more on the country in which you were born than on the segment of society your parents belong to. This also explains why most of the environmental impacts in the world today are attributable to rich consumers, primarily based in the global North. It has been estimated that the world's top 10 per cent of income earners are responsible for between 25–43 per cent of global environmental impact, whereas the footprint of the world's bottom 10 per cent of income earners is only around 3–5 per cent of the total.[88] These huge differences are not only intolerable in their own right, they also lead to an inefficient use of resources. As illustrated by the massive diversion of land and water in the global South to satisfy consumers in the global North, it is because of the gaps in purchasing power between the respective populations – that compete for the use of the same resources – that such differentials in the ecological impact of each emerge and are allowed to persist.

For all the reasons outlined above, in addition to investing in 'triple-dividend' measures, the eradication of poverty in a post-growth society should give priority to the fight against inequalities. Much can be achieved by a combination of progressive taxation and social policies, in order to mitigate market-based inequalities and ensure a fairer distribution. Such redistributive measures will not suffice, however. *Pre-distribution* measures, to build a truly inclusive economy from which no one feels excluded, are equally vital. This is what will make a society truly convivial. The world of work is where to start.

Redefining work

Work has become central to most people's lives. Those who have work dedicate most of their time to it in order to pay for their consumption. Those who don't, or who are unable to work, resent this as an injustice or as a failure of society to value what they could contribute.

And while some feel excluded from the world of work, others are overworked and overexploited, forced to work long hours to meet their needs. People in poverty, in particular, are often in informal or precarious jobs, performed under sub-standard conditions, for wages that barely allow them to survive, let alone support their family's educational, health, housing or mobility needs: globally, more than one in five workers lived in poverty before the Covid-19 pandemic,[89] and even in the European Union, there were at the time nearly 20.5 million 'working poor', constituting 10 per cent of the active working population, whose incomes do not protect them from the risk of poverty.[90]

Structural unemployment is incompatible with the idea that there is a right to work, and a corresponding duty for society to ensure that all individuals of working age who wish to work should be able to do so. It is also deeply dysfunctional. As a result of competitive pressure and of management techniques that constantly demand the individual worker improves their performance,[91] rates of burn-out or exhaustion are reaching unprecedented highs, while at the same time many who would like to work are not provided the opportunity to do so – and to therefore gain experience, perfect their skills, extend their social networks, and achieve a degree of economic independence.

Work can be a source of dignity, emancipation and pride, as well as essential to the self-fulfilment of the individual. But work today is unevenly distributed, and it is mostly not organized to further individual self-fulfilment. The vague invocation of 'merit' is used to justify unequal access to the best jobs, which are monopolized in most societies by those, more often men than women, who have the right connections,[92] and the family and educational background that prepares them best to compete.

The more unequal the country, the more the rhetoric of meritocracy is prevalent,[93] in particular among the richest groups within society, who seek to present their privileged situation as the just reward for their individual efforts.[94] In turn, however, this leads many to see personal failings as the main cause of poverty, so that people in poverty are blamed for being poor.[95] 'Meritocracy' both reduces empathy towards affected groups and makes inequality look like an inevitable and, to some extent, even desirable phenomenon – a means to incentivize people to achieve more and to relentlessly 'improve' and 'adapt' to the exigencies of the market.[96] Indeed, the more a society moves towards realizing the meritocratic ideal, the more we confront the paradox highlighted by the Harvard philosopher Michael Sandel: precisely because such a society is organized to reward 'merit', the losers will not be forgiven for their failures, and the elites (the winners) will be convinced that their successes are attributable to their efforts alone – making them blind to the remaining gaps between the meritocratic 'ideal' and the reality of unequal opportunities.[97]

Three major and complementary steps should be taken to reaffirm the nature of work as a human right and to ensure that it contributes to a life in dignity. First, a duty should be imposed on society to provide work to all those who can and are willing to work: such a 'job guarantee' would establish the state as an employer of last resort, with impacts across the whole economy. Second, workplace democracy should give workers a greater say in the organization of work and in the strategic decisions of the organization to which they belong. Third and finally, working time should be significantly reduced, to break the spend-consume cycle and increase the time available both for own-production and for civic engagement, thus also reducing the dependency on the market for the satisfaction of basic needs. In combination, these reforms will ensure that work contributes to the fulfilment of individual workers, and that we move away from the extractive form of economy that is dominant today.

THE RIGHT TO WORK

Unemployment has huge costs for both individuals and society.[98] In advanced economies that provide unemployment benefits or social aid, unemployment has to be compensated for with public funds so as to provide basic income security to the individual. These expenditures are more modest than is generally thought: in 2021, OECD countries spent an average of 0.58 per cent of GDP on unemployment benefits, although that percentage is higher in certain countries such as Finland (1.51 per cent), Spain (1.53 per cent) or France (which, with 2.79 per cent, dedicates a particularly high proportion of its revenue to compensating unemployment).[99]

In addition to those direct costs however, unemployment has a range of indirect costs, which are generally underestimated. It may compound the impacts of an economic crisis, since the decrease in demand may create the conditions for a deeper and longer-lasting recession. In local communities where layoffs take place, indirect job destruction spreads like a disease to surrounding areas, affecting whole communities.[100] High unemployment often translates into higher levels of crime: data concerning the United States between 1970 and 1993 suggest that a 2 per cent decrease of the unemployment rate reduces the number of burglaries by 9 per cent.[101] And it is society as a whole that suffers the consequences of the huge waste of talent that results from the under-employment of large segments of the active population, while it cannot even satisfy a large range of social needs.

For the unemployed themselves, not having a job results in a depletion of their skills, and in discrimination. Employers are reluctant to hire long-term unemployed candidates. They tend to interpret the fact that a person has been unemployed for long periods of time as betraying a lack of motivation.[102] They also tend to reason that, if other employers have not recruited the person seeking a job, there must be a reason for this, so that in conditions of uncertainty they will prefer not to take the chance: economists describe this particular form of risk aversion as 'rational herding'.[103] People who can't find a job face high levels of depression and anxiety.[104] Their life expectancy is reduced,[105] including because of the higher suicide rates: in New Zealand, an unemployed person is three times more likely to commit suicide than a person who has a job.[106]

Mass unemployment may appear, for some, as a convenient means to justify paying workers less. It is not an inevitable and permanent feature of the economy, however. Instead, the 'job guarantee', as it has been referred to in contemporary debates, recognizes that each individual has a right to work.[107] Its basic premise is that governments, including in particular local government, or private entities with the support of public funding, will provide a decent job to each working-age individual who seeks to work, if that individual is unable to find employment at acceptable conditions elsewhere.

The idea is not new. In the United States, the Works Progress Administration was part of the New Deal response to the depression of the 1930s. Public employment schemes have been a common response to structural unemployment in OECD countries, though with less use in recent decades.[108] The Covid-19 pandemic, which led to the large-scale deployment of furlough schemes in the countries that could afford them, led to a revival of the idea.

A society that provides a job guarantee recognizes that each individual has a valuable contribution to make to social progress. It is a society that recognizes the worthiness of each of its members, and that refuses the idea that some are redundant. It is also a society that acknowledges the distinction between employment that is created in response to demand, as expressed by the market, and employment that is created in response to societal needs, including needs that the market cannot satisfy because no household or enterprise will be able or willing to pay for the services meeting such needs. It is a society, finally, which confronts this paradox: while employment opportunities are too few to absorb all the available workforce, a range of social needs remain unfulfilled, particularly for the ecological transformation of societies or in the care economy.

We may be facing a shortage of jobs, but certainly not of work that needs to be performed. The problem is that jobs that benefit the local community or society as a whole, rather than only a specific employer, will typically only be economically viable if supported through the public purse. This is the case for jobs that establish or maintain 'commons' such as ecosystems, or projects that are accessible to all, from collective vegetable gardens to community-led energy cooperatives, public housing projects and initiatives in the sharing economy; jobs that contribute to the circular economy, encouraging the repair, reuse and recycling of consumer items; and jobs that provide care and support to groups of the population that cannot afford to pay for such support themselves – including older persons, people with disabilities or low-income households.

Guaranteeing the right to work through a job guarantee can be costly, since the jobs created will be financed by the state. Yet the immediate fiscal implications should be balanced against the enormous benefits, both for the individual and for society, of combating long-term unemployment. In addition to the savings involved – since unemployment benefits or social aid to the job-seekers can be suspended – the workers provided with employment will spend as consumers and contribute to social insurance schemes. The services they provide will benefit society, meeting needs that, in the absence of a solvent demand (that is, expressed by actors willing and able to pay), markets currently cannot respond to. This will also give meaning to their work, bringing it closer to what one scholar has described as 'socially capability-enhancing work', in contrast to dominant approaches to labour that value it only to the extent it is so-called 'productive work', that is, work valued by the market.[109]

Moreover, the introduction of a job guarantee de-commodifies labour – the immediate implication being that, in all the branches of the economy, including in the profit-driven sectors, the bargaining position of workers will be strengthened, since they have the fall-back option of seeking decent employment paid for by the public purse. In 1919, article 427 of the Treaty of Versailles stated that 'labour should not be regarded merely as a commodity or article of commerce', and this principle was again enunciated in 1944, in the International Labour Organization (ILO) Declaration of Philadelphia. It is this idea that the job guarantee will help to realize.

WORKPLACE DEMOCRACY

The second workplace reform concerns workplace democracy. This is at the heart of a manifesto launched in May 2020, at the initiative of Isabelle Ferreras, Dominique Méda and Julie Battilana, to put this idea at the heart of the post-Covid-19 economic recovery: it has now been joined by more than 6,000 researchers.[110]

Historically, the prevalent model of growth was based on a compromise: workers' wages would increase in line with productivity gains, provided they delegated the managerial functions – the power to make strategic choices within the firm – to the owners of capital.[111] Most firms have thus become autocratic institutions, organized hierarchically and dominated by the owners of capital. This limits the ability of work to provide opportunities for self-fulfilment, or what some authors have called 'the expansion of the capabilities of workers'.[112] It is also inefficient: studies show that democratically managed firms are in fact more competitive than firms that are managed technocratically, solely with a view to increasing the profits of the owners of capital.[113]

Democratizing work – for example, by establishing a 'second chamber', composed of workers' representatives alongside the management board appointed by the shareholders, with both chambers having to agree on strategic objectives[114] – would be a way to recognize the essential contribution of workers to the performance of the firm. It would ensure that the essential experience of the workers – the experiential knowledge they can contribute to deliberations – is valued, allowing more informed, and thus better, decisions to be taken. It would also ensure that firms serve not only the interests of shareholders in the maximization of short-term profits but also the interests of workers in both individual and social capability-enhancing work – so that work is meaningful to the workers themselves and to the community. It would ensure, in particular, that the environmental costs of production are not externalized to the fullest extent possible, and thus borne by the rest of society or by future generations, but are rather internalized, and that any negative impacts from the economic activity are minimized. Workers, more than shareholders living far away from where the productive activity takes place, can be presumed to care more about the impacts of such activity on their communities in both the short and long-term.

Finally, democratizing work would stem or reverse the widening gap between those earning the highest and the lowest incomes within the firm. In 2017, the ILO reported that in Europe, in the 1 per cent of firms with the highest average wages, the bottom 1 per cent of workers were paid on average €7.10 per hour while the top 1 per cent earned an average €844 per hour, or 118 times more[115] – and Europe is not the region where inequalities within enterprises are the most pronounced. Such levels of intra-firm inequalities have very little to do with the productivity of different categories of employees. They may be attributed, rather, to the bargaining power of the respective groups; to the search by each firm for improved cost-competitiveness even if it requires repressing the wages of the least qualified workers; and to the concentration of decision-making power within the firm in the hands of the top executives. All these factors could be addressed by democratizing work.

THE REDUCTION OF WORKING HOURS

The third and final component of workplace reform should be to collectively reduce working hours. Today, the historic trend towards a decrease in working hours for full-time workers has been largely interrupted in the most advanced economies. Moreover, that decrease at the level of the individual has been more than compensated for by the remarkable increase in the proportion of women taking up waged employment so that the total number of hours worked at the societal level has in fact been rising, although major differences persist between countries.

Of course, part-time work has also increased, largely as the result of a broader trend towards the flexibilization of labour and of the growth in women's employment. But this has mostly worsened gender segregation and the segmentation of the workforce in general. Part-time workers typically occupy the lowest ranks in the occupational ladder, with limited career prospects, often with non-standard contracts; and they are mostly women.

Thus, we remain trapped in work-centred societies. These are societies in which there is too little time for individuals to seek fulfilment in leisure activities or in community service and, as a result, many societal needs remain unfulfilled. And these are societies in which, because individuals cannot develop new skills through own-production activities (such as by growing their own vegetables or repairing their clothes), they remain fully dependent on the market for most goods and services they consume, leading them to have to depend on remunerated work to avoid falling into poverty.

It is especially urgent to address this, since productivity gains, now accelerated by advances in artificial intelligence and automation,[116] may lead to unemployment for workers who become redundant;[117] or to higher incomes and thus increased consumption, which risks worsening environmental destruction; or, most likely, to an unstable combination of both. The question is whether the reduction of total working time will lead to further exclusion or, instead, to a fairer distribution of both work and leisure time.

There are four main reasons why a collective and significant reduction of working hours should be a priority for a convivial and sustainable society.[118]

The first is that shorter working hours may contribute to gender equality. The massive increase of women's waged employment has allowed many women to gain economic independence. Yet at the same time many women who are waged workers shoulder a 'triple burden', as they combine work with unremunerated care and household work. Indeed, the rise in women's employment has not been accompanied by a significant change in the allocation of tasks outside the workplace. This may still be an obstacle to women taking up employment, or it may force them into part-time work, thus limiting their professional prospects and confining them to the lower-paid positions.

In itself, a collective reduction of working time should not be seen as a substitute for other policies to change gender roles and ensure a redistribution of care and household work between women and men. Such patterns have remained essentially unchanged even when both partners reduce their working hours.[119] The reduction of working time could, however, encourage more women to seek employment, since it will make work easier to combine with the other contributions of women. It would also break the dominance of the 'long working hours culture'. This culture excludes women who bear the brunt of household and caring responsibilities, particularly from senior levels of management in which 'competitive presenteeism' – as senior employees compete over who stays the longest in the office, in order to make visible their commitment to the organization – is most significant.[120]

Second, a reduction in working hours could allow workers to dedicate more time to other activities. Such activities could be for their own self-fulfilment. They could also serve community life in order to recreate, or maintain, social capital – the trust among community members that allows for collective action, for the emergence of solidarity networks and even for political mobilization at the local level.[121] Or they could provide an opportunity to learn new skills, to produce or repair consumer goods, in order to reduce dependency on the market for the acquisition of certain goods and services.

But do shorter working hours ultimately lead to such consequences? In 1930, an industrial plant of the cereal maker Kellogg located in Michigan, USA, decided to move from three eight-hour shifts to four six-hour shifts, thus reducing working hours to six hours per day, and allowing for a redistribution of work in the context of the Great Depression. The purchasing power of the workers was largely maintained thanks to an increase in the hourly wage, and the owners' conviction was that the reduction in working hours per worker would be at least partially compensated by improved productivity.

The result of this shift was that families spent more time together. People who were sick and older people were taken better care off and were less lonely. While women workers dedicated the free time they gained mainly to household activities, the men shared this time between own-production activities, such as gardening or fishing, and getting together with others. The Kellogg experiment however, while enthusiastically welcomed by all parties when it was launched, was gradually rolled back after the Second World War and finally abandoned in 1985. Benjamin Hunnicutt, who provides the most detailed study of this episode, attributes this retreat to the weight of a full-time working culture (a definition of progress as working more for higher wages, in order to be able to consume more), as well as to men's fear that moving away from a work-centred society would undermine their role within the family. Tellingly, the departments that most resisted the return to the eight-hour norm were mainly those dominated by women. Finally, with the advent of television, and the general turn of leisure activities towards the more individualized practice of watching TV, leisure was less valued in the 1950s and 1960s than it was in earlier times, when free time was mostly seen as an opportunity for activities pursued collectively with others – a use of time that is especially difficult to maintain in a context where long working hours are the norm.[122]

Thirty years ago, Juliet Schor had already alerted us to the 'work and spend' culture dominant in rich countries, and she advocated for the collective reduction of working time as a means to escape that trap.[123] What the Kellogg experiment shows is that, in order for the reduction of working time to allow an escape from this culture, the time freed up for leisure should be sufficient to allow for the acquisition of new skills and the development of own-production activities, and that the reduction in working time should be collective – taking place at societal level rather than at individual or company level. This would increase the chances of such free time being spent with others, for the construction of collective action. And it would increase the chances of free time being used not for consumption, but for production, thus reducing the dependency of each worker on income to satisfy their (and the household's) needs.

A third reason to move towards shorter working hours is that it has significant potential to reduce the pressure of economic activity on the ecosystem.[124] A study comparing 29 high-income OECD countries over the years 1970–2007 showed that a decline in working hours reduces ecological footprints in general (measured as the surface of land required to meet the food, housing, transportation, consumer goods, and services consumption, both to provide resources and to absorb waste), the carbon footprint (including the carbon embedded in imports and exports) and carbon emissions (produced within the territorial unit concerned).[125] Similarly, a study on the time-use and consumption patterns of Swedish households concluded that a decrease in working time by 1 per cent may reduce energy use and greenhouse gas emissions by about 0.7 per cent and 0.8 per cent, respectively.[126] And, in a study covering all 50 US states, Jared Fitzgerald, Juliet Schor and Andrew Jorgenson found a significant relationship between long working hours and carbon emissions: this relationship is attributable both to the contribution of long working hours to GDP and to the more carbon-intensive lifestyles of workers facing time-poverty because of long working hours.[127]

Most of these environmental gains form working-time reduction are because of the effects of lower income and thus lower consumption. In contrast, long working hours, especially combined with productivity gains, result in higher incomes and thus increased consumption: this contributes to the 'work and spend' cycle denounced by Juliet Schor that currently fuels economic growth. Reducing working hours is a way to break this vicious cycle, in which people work more in order to consume more and can afford to consume more because they work more. In the specialized literature, this is called the 'scale effect' (or the 'wealth effect') of long working hours: the longer you work, the more you consume.

At the same time, as individuals increase their leisure time, they can opt for more time-consuming ways of satisfying their needs. They may use slower but less energy-intensive modes of transportation, for instance, opting to travel by bicycle or by public transport rather than by car; they may prepare their own food rather than buying prepared meals or eating out; they may invest more in own-production or in sharing initiatives with their immediate neighbours.[128] This is called the 'composition effect' (or 'time-use effect') of working hours: longer working hours go hand in hand with hurried lifestyles that force people to opt for time-saving products or technologies, even though these are generally more energy-intensive.[129]

There are dilemmas involved in the reduction of working hours. If the aim is to reduce fatigue for workers, without diminishing their standard of living, working-time reduction should go hand in hand with the recruitment of additional workers – since the risk, otherwise, would be greater intensification of work – and it should leave wages intact. That would also ensure that working-time reduction would help to reduce unemployment, leading to a fairer distribution of work.[130]

This, however, would significantly limit the positive impacts expected from working-time reduction on environmental sustainability. Indeed, the 'scale effect' of working-time reduction (the reduced consumption linked to people working less) is far more significant than the 'composition effect' (the use of leisure time to increase time-consuming but energy-saving activities).[131] In other words, the principal contribution of reduced working hours to sustainability is that, if it reduces GDP, this results in lower consumption. If instead reducing working hours does not reduce the GDP, allowing existing levels of spending to be maintained, the impacts on the environment will be far less significant.

While this is a real dilemma, it can be eased, partly at least, by the adoption of three complementary measures. First, by strengthening workplace democracy as this would avoid working-time reduction leading to greater intensification of work, which negatively impacts the health of workers. Second, by redistributive measures, including a flattening of the wages between the highest and the lowest wage earners at firm level:[132] this would at least put a minimal brake on the most unsustainable forms of consumption that the highest wage earners can indulge in. Third, by relying on a new narrative that shifts the focus to well-being and happiness as a more desirable alternative to increased possibilities of material consumption in the search for happiness: while the reduction of working time may lead to better-paid workers' incomes being slightly reduced, shorter working hours could be seen as a partial compensation for that loss, since the time freed up for life outside work – time affluence – reduces consumption desire and environmental impact.

Individuals with more time affluence are better equipped to enjoy the present moment. They enjoy a greater sense of autonomy and competence. They engage more in intimate relationships. They can pursue activities related to personal growth, connections with others and physical fitness.[133] It should, therefore, not come as a surprise that in rich countries workers increasingly express a preference for working less, even if this means earning less:[134] their life satisfaction increases with shorter working hours.[135]

Conclusion

A time will come when historians of the future will see our insistence on increasing GDP as some odd fixation, a bizarre diversion from the real concerns of people. The quest for GDP growth benefits the largest and most competitive economic actors: these champions of mass production are the winners. It hurts the least qualified workers and the less competitive businesses: they are the losers. And people in poverty only gain under a very specific set of conditions: if growth leads to increased public revenue, if that revenue serves to finance public services and social protection, and if they have effective access to both.

That is not to say that economic growth is per se a bad thing. The problem is not growth as such. It is, rather, the ideology of *growthism*: the mistaken belief that all the challenges of society can be met if, and only if, we first increase monetary wealth, as measured in GDP terms.[1] To us, what should matter is not growth: it should be the health of ecosystems, of individuals and of communities; the strengthening of social capital; well-being in all its dimensions; our ability to flourish. Whether the increase of GDP will help or not depends on how such increase is achieved, and if it does occur, how it will be used.

Economic growth is still indispensable for alleviating poverty in low-income countries, provided it is spread equally and provided wealth creation serves primarily to finance public services and strengthen social protection. But the search for growth in more affluent countries has now become counter-productive: its boasted benefits have long been overshadowed by its corrosive impacts on society and on the environment. And in no society will poverty automatically disappear with general economic progress. As long as we insist on defining such 'progress' as the increase of material wealth, we will continue, in the very name of realizing this objective, to build an extractive economy: one that exhausts the ecosystems and the individual, and that tolerates rising inequalities.

General economic progress as it is currently conceived may change the face of poverty, it may 'modernize' it – but it will not succeed in eradicating it. More audacity and more imagination are needed. We need to invest in technologies and infrastructure. We need to develop business models that encourage forms of production that are more labour-intensive and less energy-intensive, and we need to ensure that the scarce resources we can use will provide the goods and services essential to a decent life at a price that makes them affordable for all.

We need to stop seeing growth as a substitute for redistribution, and we need to stop seeing the combination of work and consumption as a substitute for human flourishing. We need to make space for activities that promote the well-being of all individuals and their capacity for own-production, thus limiting dependency on markets. And we need to put a brake on, and then reverse, the trends towards universal commodification, which leads market mechanisms to penetrate into all spheres of life – thus worsening the exclusion of those with a limited ability to pay.

A growing number of social movements are now endorsing this vision. They are joined by scientists who are working on the contours of the post-growth economy and on how to escape the temptation to see the increase of monetary wealth as the only way for societies to address the challenges they face. It is time that governments took notice and put the twentieth century behind them.

Notes

Note: All URLs last consulted on 9 December 2023.

Preface

1. These data are based on Angus Maddison, *The World Economy*, vol. 1: *A Millennial Perspective* (Paris: OECD, 2006), pp. 128, 132 and 138.

2. The expression 'the Great Acceleration' was initially put forward in the first synthesis report of the International Geosphere-Biosphere Programme (IGBP), led by Will Steffen: Will Steffen et al., *IGBP First Synthesis, Global Change and the Earth System: A Planet under Pressure* (Berlin: Springer-Verlag, 2004). This research sought to link socio-economic trends, such as the rise of income per capita or the growth of the volumes of international trade and investment to Earth System indicators, such as the erosion of biodiversity, the concentration of greenhouse gases in the atmosphere or the extraction of mineral resources. For an undated version, see Will Steffen, Wendy Broadgate, Lisa Deutsch, Owen Gaffney and Cornelia Ludwig, 'The trajectory of the Anthropocene: The Great Acceleration', *Anthropocene Review* 2(1) (2015), pp. 81–98.

3. Guy Standing, *The Precariat: The New Dangerous Class*, 2nd edn (London: Bloomsbury, 2011).

4. Kate Raworth, *Doughnut Economics: Seven Ways to Think Like a 21st-century Economist* (London: Chelsea Green Publishing, 2017). The framework was initially designed by Raworth in 2012, in a report she prepared for Oxfam: *A Safe and Just Space for Humanity: Can We Live within the Doughnut?* (Oxford: Oxfam, 2012). See https://doughnuteconomics.org

5. Jason Hickel, *Less Is More: How Degrowth Will Save the World* (London: Penguin House, 2020).

6. Clive Hamilton, *Growth Fetish* (London: Pluto Press, 2004), p. 3.
7. The expression 'social capital' was made popular by the best-selling book of the Harvard sociologist Robert Putnam, who defines the notion as 'connections among individuals – social networks and the norms of reciprocity and trustworthiness that arise from them'. See Robert Putnam, *Bowling Alone: The Collapse and Revival of American Community* (New York: Simon & Schuster, 2000), p. 19. The Social Capital Initiative of the World Bank had preceded the book, however: it was an attempt by the Bank, launched in 1996, to assess the impact of social capital on the success of development projects. See also World Bank, *World Development Report 1997: The State in a Changing World* (Washington, DC: World Bank Group, 1997), p. 114 (noting that: 'The debate about the contribution of social capital to economic and social development is just beginning, and the early evidence is by no means unambiguous. But some studies are already demonstrating its potential impact on local economic development, on the provision of local public goods, and on the performance of public agencies').
8. Cornelius Castoriadis, *Les carrefours du labyrinthe*, vol. 1 (Paris: Seuil, 2017 [1978]), p. 141.

Introduction

1. OECD, *A Broken Social Elevator? How to Promote Social Mobility* (Paris: OECD, 2018), p. 26.
2. Ibid.
3. Quoted in Tim Jackson, *Post Growth: Life after Capitalism* (London: Polity, 2021), p. 24.
4. See: www.ons.gov.uk/peoplepopulationandcommunity/personal andhouseholdfinances/incomeandwealth/bulletins/household disposableincomeandinequality/yearending2018
5. Economic growth is measured by an indicator, GDP, which captures the total output of the economy, or what was initially referred to as 'national income'. The first version of the indicator was designed by the economist Simon Kuznets in 1933, acting at the request of US President Franklin Delano Roosevelt: it was con-

sidered important at the time to measure whether the US economy was performing well to erase the impacts of the Great Depression. Since that early period, statisticians have agreed on harmonized methods to measure GDP, allowing for cross-country comparisons. A highly readable account of the rise of GDP as the key indicator of an economy's performance is by David Pilling, *The Growth Delusion: Wealth, Poverty, and the Well-Being of Nations* (New York: Tim Duggan Books, 2018).

6. Dominique Méda, *La mystique de la croissance: comment s'en libérer* (Paris: Flammarion, 2014).

7. See e.g. Tim Jackson, *Prosperity without Growth: Economics for a Finite Planet* (London: Routledge, 2009) (based on the 2009 report authored by Tim Jackson for the UK's Sustainable Development Commission under the title *Prosperity without Growth? The Transition to a Sustainable Economy*). See also the updated and revised edition published in 2017, *Prosperity without Growth: Foundations for the Economy of Tomorrow* (London: Routledge, 2017); Giorgos Kallis, 'In defence of degrowth', *Ecological Economics* 70(5) (2011), pp. 873–80; Isabelle Cassiers, Kevin Maréchal and Dominique Méda (eds), *Post-growth Economics and Society: Exploring the Paths of a Social and Ecological Transition* (London: Routledge, 2018); Hickel, *Less Is More*.

1   What is Poverty?

1. See https://unstats.un.org/sdgs/report/2022/The-Sustainable-Development-Goals-Report-2022.pdf

2. See *The Parlous State of Poverty Eradication*, Report of the Special Rapporteur on extreme poverty and human rights, Philip Alston, to 44th session of the Human Rights Council (A/HRC/44/40) (2020).

3. The dollar-a-day approach was initially proposed in 1991 by a team within the World Bank led by Martin Ravallion. Their intention was to estimate poverty across developing countries for the year 1985, and to adopt a measure independent from any country-specific (national) poverty line, in order to allow for cross-country comparisons. Using 1985 PPP exchange rates and

THE POVERTY OF GROWTH

data on the national poverty lines from a group of 33 developing and developed countries, the team relied on an econometric model that concluded that a $0.76-a-day minimum absolute poverty line (in 1985 prices) might be an appropriate tool for that purpose. The 'one-dollar per day' PPP international poverty line corresponded approximately, at the time, to the 'absolute' component of the national poverty lines set by Indonesia, Bangladesh, Nepal, Kenya, Tanzania, Morocco, the Philippines and Pakistan. In other words, the premise of this approach is that national poverty lines consist of two components: the absolute, which is fixed through time and countries and corresponds to the basic needs of the individual (essentially, what is needed in order not to starve), and the relative component, which evolves as a result of economic development, increasing as the average wealth within the population rises. The 'absolute' component is grounded in the idea that individuals have certain 'basic needs' to satisfy, which the International Labour Organization (ILO) defined as follows: 'First, certain minimum requirements of a family for private consumption: adequate food, shelter and clothing, as well as certain household equipment and furniture. Second, they include essential services provided by and for the community at large, such as safe drinking water, sanitation, public transport and health, educational and cultural facilities.' ILO, *Target Setting for Basic Needs* (Geneva: ILO, 1982), p. 6. This initial measure of extreme poverty was re-examined in 2009 to take into account the national poverty lines of a broader set of countries (75 instead of 33 in the original sample), and to rely on 2005 PPP exchange rates. This led to the international poverty line of US$1.25 a day that was used to define the target associated with SDG1. See Martin Ravallion, Chen Shaohua and Prem Sangraula, 'Dollar a day revisited', *World Bank Economic Review* 23(2) (2009), pp. 163–84. This measure corresponds to the mean poverty line of the group of countries (a total of 15) with average personal consumption expenditure below $60 per month. These were, starting from the country with the lowest personal consumption expenditure: Malawi, Mali, Ethiopia, Sierra Leone, Niger, Uganda, Gambia,

Rwanda, Guinea-Bissau, Tanzania, Tajikistan, Mozambique, Chad, Nepal and Ghana.

4. This measure relies on the same sample of the national poverty lines of 15 poor countries, using 2011 PPP exchange rates. See Francisco H.G. Ferreira, Shaohua Chen, Andrew Dabalen, Yuri Dikhanov, Nada Hamadeh, Dean Jolliffe et al., 'A global count of the extreme poor in 2012: Data issues, methodology and initial results', *Journal of Economic Inequality* 14 (2016), pp. 141–72.

5. Martin Ravallion, *Poverty Lines in Theory and Practice*, Living Standards Measurement Study Working Paper (Washington, DC: World Bank, 1998), p. 133.

6. This oversimplifies a complex debate between 'absolute' and 'relative' definitions of poverty. For a nuanced view, see Amartya K. Sen, 'Poor, relatively speaking', *Oxford Economic Papers* 35 (1983), pp. 153–69.

7. See Daryl Collins, Jonathan Morduch, Stuart Rutherford and Orlanda Ruthven, *Portfolios of the Poor* (Princeton, NJ: Princeton University Press, 2009) (based on studies in India, Bangladesh and South Africa, finding that medical, wedding and funeral expenses are most likely to cause catastrophic disruption to orderly financial planning in highly straitened circumstances).

8. Peter Townsend, *Poverty in the United Kingdom: A Survey of Household Resources and Standards of Living* (Berkeley, CA; University of California Press, 1979).

9. Amartya K. Sen, *Commodities and Capabilities* (Amsterdam: North-Holland, 1985, repr. Oxford University Press, 1997).

10. On the notion of the multidimensional understanding of poverty and its value, see in particular Sabina Alkire, James. E. Foster, Suman Seth, Maria Emma Santos, Jose M. Roche and Paola Ballon, *Multidimensional Poverty Measurement and Analysis* (Oxford: Oxford University Press, 2015); and the report coordinated by Anthony Atkinson for the World Bank, *Monitoring Global Poverty: Report of the Commission on Global Poverty* (Washington, DC: World Bank, 2017).

11. Programme of Action adopted at the 1995 World Summit for Social Development, para. 19. See: www.un.org/development/

desa/dspd/world-summit-for-social-development-1995/wssd-1995-agreements.html (accessed 4 December 2023).

12. Committee on Economic, Social and Cultural Rights, Statement on poverty adopted on 4 May 2001 (E/C.12/2001/10), para. 8.

13. Although the emphasis has generally been on economic, social and cultural rights in the discussion of poverty-reduction policies, people in poverty also face systematic violations of their civil and political rights, including as a result of police brutality, excessive subjection to pre-trial detention, and a denial of voting rights. See Report of the Special Rapporteur on extreme poverty and human rights presented to the 72nd session of the General Assembly (A/72/502) (4 October 2017).

14. Paul Dolan, Tessa Peasgood and Mathew White, 'Do we really know what makes us happy? A review of the economic literature on the factors associated with subjective well-being', *Journal of Economic Psychology* 29 (2008), pp. 94–122; Sara J. Solnick and David Hemenway, 'Is more always better? A survey on positional concerns', *Journal of Economic Behavior & Organization* 37 (1998), pp. 373–83.

15. Deepa Narayan, Robert Chambers, Meera Shah and Patti Petesch, *Voices of the Poor: Crying Out for Change* (Oxford: Oxford University Press, 2000).

16. See Rachel Bray, Marianne de Laat, Xavier Godinot, Alberto Ugarte and Robert Walker, 'Realising poverty in all its dimensions: A six-country participatory study', *World Development* 134 (2020). ATD stands for 'All Together in Dignity'.

17. Ibid.

18. Ibid.

2 Is Economic Growth the Solution?

1. Under SDG8, which relates to decent work and economic growth, target 8.1 is to 'sustain per capita economic growth in accordance with national circumstances and, in particular, at least 7 per cent gross domestic product growth per annum in the least developed countries'. The associated indicator (8.1.1), is the annual growth rate of real GDP per capita.

2. Elizabeth Farina, Graciela E. Gutman, Pablo José Lavarello, Rubens Nunes and Thomas Reardon, 'Private and public milk standards in Argentina and Brazil', *Food Policy* 30 (2005), pp. 302–15.

3. Thomas Reardon, C. Peter Timmer and Bart Minten, 'Supermarket revolution in Asia and emerging development strategies to include small farmers', *Proceedings of the National Academy of Sciences* 109(31) (2010), pp. 12332–7, www.pnas.org/cgi/doi/10.1073/pnas.1003160108.

4. United Kingdom Competition Commission, *The Supply of Groceries in the UK Market Investigation* (2008), para. 5.27; and Paul W. Dobson and Roman Inderst, 'Differential buyer power and the waterbed effect: Do strong buyers benefit or harm consumers?', *European Competition Law Review* 28 (2007), p. 393.

5. P. Gibbon, *The Commodity Question: New Thinking on Old Problems*, Occasional Paper 2005/13 (New York: Human Development Report Office).

6. Richard Easterlin, 'Does economic growth improve the human lot? Some empirical evidence', in *Nations and Households in Economic Growth* (Stanford, CA: Stanford University Press, 1972); Richard Easterlin, 'Will raising the incomes of all increase the happiness of all?', *Journal of Economic Behaviour and Organization* 27 (1995), pp. 35–47; and Richard Layard, *Happiness: Lessons from a New Science* (London: Penguin Books, 2005).

7. Eloi Laurent and Jacques Le Cacheux, *Un nouveau monde économique: mesurer le bien-être et la soutenabilité au XXIème siècle* (Paris: Odile Jacob, 2015), pp. 23–5.

8. The notion of counter-productivity is borrowed from Ivan Illich, but I expand it here beyond the areas (education, health and mobility) to which Illich sought to apply it. See, in particular, Ivan Illich, *Deschooling Society* (London: Calder and Boyars, 1971); and Ivan Illich, *Medical Nemesis: The Expropriation of Health* (London: Calder and Boyars, 1975).

9. John M. Keynes, 'Economic possibilities for our grandchildren', in *Essays in Persuasion* (New York: Harcourt Brace, 1932), pp. 365–6.

10. John K. Galbraith, *The Affluent Society* (Boston, MA: Houghton Mifflin Co., 1958), ch. 11.

11. Joseph Stiglitz, Amartya Sen and Jean-Paul Fitoussi, *Report by the Commission on the Measurement of Economic Performance and Social Progress* (2009), p. 8, https://ec.europa.eu/eurostat/documents/8131721/8131772/Stiglitz-Sen-Fitoussi-Commission-report.pdf

12. Tim Jackson, *Prosperity without Growth: Foundations for the Economy of Tomorrow* (London: Routledge, 2017), p. 57; Richard Wilkinson and Kate Pickett, *The Inner Level: How More Equal Societies Reduce Stress, Restore Sanity and Improve Everyone's Well-being* (London: Allen Lane, 2018), p. 226.

13. Albert Hirschman and Michael Rothschild, 'The changing tolerance for income inequality in the course of economic development', *Quarterly Journal of Economics* 87(4) (1973), pp. 544–66.

14. George Loewenstein, 'Anticipation and the valuation of delayed consumption', *Economic Journal*, 97(387) (1987), pp. 666–84; Claudia Senik, 'Is man doomed to progress? Expectations, adaptation and well-being', *Journal of Economic Behaviour and Organization* 68(1) (2008), pp. 140–52.

15. For a fuller discussion, see Claudia Senik, *L'économie du bonheur* (Paris: Seuil, 'La République des Idées', 2014).

16. Fred Hirsch, *Social Limits to Growth* (London: Routledge, 1977), p. 36.

17. Harry Brighouse and Adam Swift, 'Equality, priority and positional goods', *Ethics* 116(3) (2006), pp. 471–97.

18. Tibor Scitovsky, *The Joyless Economy: The Psychology of Human Satisfaction* (Oxford: Oxford University Press, 1992, rev. edn [1976]).

19. Albert Hirschman, *Shifting Involvements: Private Interest and Public Action* (Princeton, NJ: Princeton University Press, 1982), pp. 32–8.

20. See Robert H. Lustig, *The Hacking of the American Mind: The Science Behind the Corporate Takeover of Our Bodies and Brains* (New York: Simon & Schuster, 2017).

21. Richard Layard, *Happiness: Lessons from a New Science* (London: Penguin Books, 2005).

22. See above, fn. 2.

23. In the United Kingdom, people living in the most deprived 10 per cent of regions faced 41 per cent higher levels of concentration of nitrous oxide from industrial activity and transport. See K. Lucas et al., *Environment and Social Justice: Rapid Research and Evidence Review*, Final Report (London: Defra, 2004).

24. Service for the fight against poverty, precarity and social exclusion (Belgium), *Sustainability and Poverty (Durabilité et pauvreté)*, Biannual report 2018–19 (Brussels, 2019), p. 13.

25. Robert Bullard et al., *Toxic Wastes and Race at Twenty, 1987–2007: Grassroots Struggles to Dismantle Environmental Racism in the United States* (Cleveland, OH: United Church of Christ Justice and Witness Ministry, Cleveland, 2007); Rachel Morello-Frosh et al., 'Environmental justice and southern California's "risks-cape": The distribution of air toxic exposures and health risks among diverse communities', *Urban Affairs Review* 36(4) (2001), pp. 551–78; Lisa Schweitzer and Jianping Zhou, 'Neighborhood air quality, respiratory health, and vulnerable populations in compact and sprawled regions', *Journal of the American Planning Association* 76(3) (2010), pp. 363–71.

26. Convention on Biological Diversity, COP 12 Decision XII/5 (2014), annex, para. 1.

27. Helen Suich, Caroline Howe and Georgina Mace, 'Ecosystem services and poverty alleviation: A review of the empirical links', *Ecosystem Services* 12 (2015), pp. 137–47.

28. ILO, *World Employment and Social Outlook 2018: Greening with Jobs* (Geneva: ILO, 2018), p. 7.

29. ILO, *Indigenous Peoples and Climate Change: From Victims to Change Agents through Decent Work* (Geneva: ILO, 2017).

30. See *Climate Change and Poverty*, Report of the Special Rapporteur on extreme poverty and human rights, Philip Alston, to the 41st session of the Human Rights Council (A/HRC/41/39) (2019).

31. The expression was initially coined in 2009 by a group of 28 scientists brought together by Johan Rockström from the Stockholm Resilience Centre: Johan Rockström, Will Steffen et al., 'A safe operating space for humanity', *Nature* 461 (2009), pp. 472–5. The approach was updated and refined in 2015 (see Will Steffen,

Katherine Richardson, Johan Rockström, Sarah E. Cornell et al., 'Planetary boundaries: Guiding human development on a changing planet', *Science* 347(6223) (2015), doi: 10.1126/science.1259855. The most recent updating took place in September 2023, by which time it was estimated that six of the nine initial planetary boundaries had been crossed: see Katherine Richardson, Will Steffen, Wolfgang Lucht, Jorgen Bendtsen, Sarah E. Cornell, Jonathan F. Donges et al., 'Earth beyond six of nine planetary boundaries', *Science Advances* 9(7) (2023), p. 37, doi: 10.1126/sciadv.adh2458.

32. Rio+20 Conference on Sustainable Development, *The Future We Want*, Outcome document of the UN Conference on Sustainable Development (A/CONF.216/L), paras 4 and 12, refer to 'sustained, inclusive and equitable economic growth'.

33. Ibid., para. 56.

34. Jason Hickel and Giorgos Kallis, 'Is green growth possible?', *New Political Economy* 25(4) (2019), pp. 469–86, doi: 10.1080/13563467.2019.1598964.

35. The early twenty-first century witnessed an increase in resource consumption that is more significant than the increase in GDP: Fridolin Krausmann et al., 'Growth in global materials use, GDP and population during the 20th century', *Ecological Economics* 68(10) (2009), pp. 2696–705.

36. Thomas Wiedmann, Heinz Schandl, Manfred Lenzen, Daniel Moran, Sangwon Suh, James West et al., 'The material footprint of nations', *Proceedings of the National Academy of Sciences of the United States of America*, 112(20) (2013), pp. 6271–6. On the importance of distinguishing consumption-based carbon emissions (taking into account emissions embodied in imports) and production-based (territorial) carbon emissions, see Harry C. Wilting and Kees Vringer, 'Carbon and land use accounting from a producer's and consumer's perspective – an empirical examination covering the world', *Economic Systems Research* 21(3) (2009), pp. 291–310; and Nadim Ahmad and Andrew Wyckoff, *Carbon Dioxide Emissions Embodied in International Trade of Goods*, OECD Science, Technology and Industry Working Papers, 2003/15 (Paris: OECD, 2003).

37. Giorgos Kallis, 'Radical dematerialization and degrowth', *Philosophical Transactions of the Royal Society A: Mathematical, Physical and Engineering Sciences* 375 (2017).

38. Timothée Parrique, Jonathan Barth, François Briens, Christian Kerschner, Alejo Kraus-Polk, Anna Kuokkanen et al., *Decoupling Debunked: Evidence and Arguments against Green Growth as a Sole Strategy for Sustainability* (Brussels: European Environmental Bureau, 2019), p. 31.

39. Corrine Le Quéré, Jan Iver Korsbakken, Charlie Wilson et al., 'Drivers of declining CO_2 emissions in 18 developed economies', *Nature Climate Change* 9 (2019), pp. 213–17.

40. Jefim Vogel and Jason Hickel, 'Is green growth happening? An empirical analysis of achieved versus Paris-compliant CO–GDP decoupling in high-income countries', *Lancet Planet Health* 7(9) (2023), e759–e769.

41. See J. Daniel Khazzoom, 'Economic implications of mandated efficiency standards for household appliances', *The Energy Journal* 1 (1980), pp. 21–40; Leonard G. Brookes, 'The greenhouse effect: The fallacies in the energy efficiency solution', *Energy Policy* 18 (1990), pp. 199–201; Stig-Olof Holm and Gunnar Englund, 'Increased ecoefficiency and gross rebound effect: Evidence from USA and six European countries 1960–2002', *Ecological Economics* 68(3) (2009), pp. 879–87; Angela Druckman, Mona Chitnis, Steve Sorrell and Tim Jackson, 'Missing carbon reductions? Exploring rebound and backfire effects in UK households', *Energy Policy,* 39 (2011), pp. 3572–81.

42. Mona Chitnis, Steve Sorrell, Angela Druckman, Steven K. Firth and Tim Jackson, 'Who rebounds most? Estimating direct and indirect rebound effects for different UK socioeconomic groups', *Ecological Economics,* 106 (2014), pp. 12–32.

43. Mona Chitnis, Steve Sorrell, Angela Druckman, Steven K. Firth, Tim Jackson, 'Turning lights into flights: Estimating direct and indirect rebound effects for UK households', *Energy Policy,* 55 (2013), pp. 234–50.

44. Uzma Khan, Ravi Dhar and Svenja Schmidt, 'Giving consumers license to enjoy luxury', *MIT Sloan Management Review* (2010), https://sloanreview.mit.edu/article/giving-consumers-li-

cense-to-enjoy-luxury/ ('When individuals have had a chance to boost their self-image by, for example, a virtuous act, they are subsequently more likely to engage in self-indulgent consumption'); Sophie Clot, Gilles Groleau, Lisette Ibanez and Peguy Ndodjang, 'L'effet de compensation morale ou comment les bonnes actions peuvent aboutir à une situation indésirable', *Revue économique* 65(3) (2014), pp. 557–72.

45. Clot et al., 'L'effet de compensation morale ou comment les bonnes actions peuvent aboutir à une situation indésirable'.

46. Parrique et al., *Decoupling Debunked*, p. 4.

47. Global aviation today accounts for 2.5 per cent of CO_2 emissions (and 1.9 per cent of total greenhouse gas emissions). This percentage has been increasing only slightly over the years, despite the considerable increase in the volume of activity (the revenue passenger kilometres [RPK] travelled have increased almost 300-fold since 1950, and 75-fold since 1960), which illustrates the efficiency gains in the industry. However, the total contribution of aviation to radiative forcing is higher (about 3.5 per cent) once we take into account other (non-CO_2-related) contributions of aviation to global warming, in particular as a result of water-vapor trails from aircraft exhausts, contributing to cirrus cloudiness. See David S. Lee, David W. Fahey, Agnieszka Skowron et al., 'The contribution of global aviation to anthropogenic climate forcing for 2000 to 2018', *Atmospheric Environment* 244 (2021), 117834; and Hannah Ritchie, 'Climate change and flying: What share of global CO_2 emissions come from aviation?', OurWorldInData. org (October 2020).

48. The notion was put forward in a 2013 study by the consultancy firm Ernst & Young, *Hitting the Sweet Spot: The Growth of the Middle Class in Emerging Markets* (London: Ernst & Young, 2013), and discussed further in a 2017 study from the World Resources Institute; see Samantha Putt del Pino, Eliot Metzger, Deborah Drew and Kevin Moss, *The Elephant in the Boardroom: Why Unchecked Consumption is not an Option in Tomorrow's Markets* (Washington, DC: World Resources Institute, 2017).

49. The global middle class has grown significantly in recent years. Based on the standard definition of the middle class – individ-

uals who have a spending capacity of between $11 and $110 per day PPP – more than half of the world's population since 2018 live in middle-class or wealthy households. By 2018, 3.6 billion individuals belonged to this 'middle class'. This was the result of an exponential increase, from 1 billion in the late 1980s and 2 billion in 2010. See www.caixabankresearch. com/en/economics-markets/labour-market-demographics/ emergence-middle-class-emerging-country-phenomenon

50. Mobility, in particular, has increased even faster than income, leading to the emergence of a global tourism industry that is no longer limited to the affluent West: Manfred Lenzen, Ya-Yen Sun, Futu Faturay, Arne Geschke and Arunima Malik, 'The carbon footprint of global tourism', *Nature Climate Change* 8 (2018), pp. 522–8.

51. Marina Fischer-Kowalski, Mark Swilling, Ernst Ulrich von Weizsäcker, Yong Ren Yuichi Moriguchi, Wendy Crane, Fridolin Krausmann et al., *A Report of the Working Group on Decoupling Natural Resource Use and Environmental Impacts from Economic Growth* (Nairobi, Kenya: UN Environment Programme, International Resource Panel, 2011).

52. Hao Xiao, Ke-Juan Sun, Hui-Min Bi and Jin-Jin Xue, 'Changes in carbon intensity globally and in countries: Attribution and decomposition analysis', *Applied Energy* 235 (2019), pp. 1492–504.

53. Thomas Wiedmann, Manfred Lenzen, Lorenz T. Keyßer et al., 'Scientists' warning on affluence', *Nature Communications* 11 (2020), p. 3107.

54. Parrique et al., *Decoupling Debunked*, Executive Summary.

55. Helga Dittmar, 'The costs of consumer culture and the "cage within": The impact of the material "good life" and "body perfect" ideals on individuals' identity and well-being', *Psychological Inquiry* 18 (2007), pp. 23–31. Helga Dittmar, *Consumer Culture, Identity and Well-being: The Search for the 'Good Life' and the 'Body Perfect'* (Hove, UK: Psychology Press, 2007).

56. On this notion, see Mihaly Csikszentmihalyi, *Flow: The Psychology of Happiness* (London: Rider, 1992); Mihaly Csikszentmihalyi, *Finding Flow: The Psychology of Engagement with Everyday Life* (New York: Basic Books, 1997).

57. Mihaly Csikszentmihalyi, Ronald Graef and Susan McManama Gianinno, 'Energy consumption in leisure and perceived happiness', in Mihaly Csikszentmihalyi (ed.), *Flow and the Foundations of Positive Psychology* (Dordrecht: Springer, 2014), pp. 127–33; Amy Isham, Birgitta Gatersleben and Tim Jackson, 'Flow activities as a route to living well with less', *Environment and Behavior* 5(4) (2019), pp. 431–61.

58. Doris Fuchs, Marlyne Sahakian, Tobias Gumbert, Antonietta Di Giulio, Michael Maniates, Sylvia Lorek et al., *Consumption Corridors: Living a Good Life within Sustainable Limits* (London: Routledge, 2021), p. 69. See also Antonietta Di Giulio and Doris Fuchs, 'Sustainable consumption corridors: Concept, objections, and responses', *GAIA – Ecological Perspectives for Science and Society* 23 (2014), pp. 184–92.

59. Service for the fight against poverty, precarity and social exclusion (Belgium), *Sustainability and Poverty (Durabilité et pauvreté)*, pp. 98–9.

60. Eduardo Galeano, *The Open Veins of Latin America: Five Centuries of the Pillage of a Continent* (New York: Monthly Review Press, 1971).

61. On the impact of Prebisch and his continued relevance, see in particular Matias E. Margulis (ed.), *The Global Political Economy of Raúl Prebisch* (London: Routledge, 2017); and Edgar J. Dosman, *The Life and Times of Raúl Prebisch* (London: Queen's School of Policy Studies, 2008).

62. Anne Case and Angus Deaton, *Deaths of Despair and the Future of Capitalism* (Princeton, NJ: Princeton University Press, 2020). On the impact of globalization on inequalities, see generally Branko Milanovic, *Global Inequality: A New Approach for the Age of Globalization* (Cambridge, MA: Harvard University Press, 2016).

63. The correlation has been demonstrated based on the example of the granting of Permanent Normal Trade Relations (PNTR) to China in October 2000, a change that differentially exposed US counties to increased international competition. See Justin R. Pierce and Peter K. Schott, 'Trade liberalization and mortality: Evidence from US counties', *American Economic Review: Insights* 2(1) (2020), pp. 47–64.

64. Olivier De Schutter, Johan F. Swinnen and Jan Wouters (eds), *Foreign Direct Investment and Human Development: The Law and Economics of International Investment Agreements* (London: Routledge, 2012).

65. Robert L. Heilbroner, *The Nature and Logic of Capitalism* (New York: W.W. Norton, 1985), p. 60.

66. These and other examples are discussed in two books that appeared simultaneously: Michael Sandel, *What Money Can't Buy: The Moral Limits of Markets* (London: Allen Lane, 2012), and Arlie Russell Hochschild, *The Outsourced Self: What Happens When We Pay Others to Live Our Lives for Us* (New York: Metropolitan Books, 2012).

67. Ronald H. Coase, 'The problem of social cost', *Journal of Law and Economics* 3 (1960), pp. 1–44.

68. Richard Titmuss, *The Gift Relationship: From Human Blood to Social Policy* (London: Allen & Unwin, London, 1970).

69. Bruno S. Frey and Felix Oberholzer-Gee, 'The cost of price incentives: An empirical analysis of motivation crowding-out', *American Economic Review* 87(4) (1997), pp. 746–55.

70. Uri Gneezy and Aldo Rustichini, 'Pay enough or don't pay at all', *Quarterly Journal of Economics* 115(3) (2000), pp. 791–810.

71. As a result, the expansion of freedom of contract may restrict, rather than expand, the real freedom of the individual, since that individual will be exposed to coercion in market relationships. See generally Robert L. Hale, 'Coercion and distribution in a supposedly non-coercive state', *Political Science Quarterly* 38 (1923), p. 470.

72. Daniel Hausknost, 'The environmental state and the glass ceiling of transformation', *Environmental Politics* 29 (2020), pp. 17–37.

73. The most influential early contributions to this revival are Elinor Ostrom, *Governing the Commons: The Evolution of Institutions for Collective Action* (Cambridge: Cambridge University Press, 1990); David Bollier, 'The growth of the commons paradigm', in Charlotte Hess and Elinor Ostrom (eds), *Understanding Knowledge as a Commons: From Theory to Practice* (London: MIT Press, 2007), pp. 27–40; Ugo Mattei, *Beni comuni: un manifesto* (Bari:

Laterza, 2011); Pierre Dardot and Christian Laval, *Commun: essai sur la révolution au XXIème siècle* (Paris: La Découverte, 2015).

74. Martin Gilens, *Affluence and Influence: Economic Inequality and Political Power in America* (Princeton, NJ: Princeton University Press, 2012); Martin Gilens and Benjamin I. Page, 'Testing theories of American politics: Elites, interest groups, and average citizens', *Perspectives on Politics* 12(3) (2014), pp. 564–81.

75. Joseph Stiglitz, *The Price of Inequality* (New York: W.W. Norton, 2013); Lee Drutman, *The Business of America is Lobbying: How Corporations became Politicized and Politics became More Corporate* (Oxford: Oxford University Press, 2015).

76. Wade Cole, 'Poor and powerless: Economic and political inequality in cross-national perspective, 1981–2011', *International Sociology* 33(3) (2018), pp. 21–2.

77. Susan George, *Shadow Sovereigns: How Global Corporations are Seizing Power* (Cambridge: Polity Press, 2015).

78. UNCTAD, *Beyond Austerity: Towards a Global New Deal*, UNCTAD Trade and Development Report 2017 (New York: UN, 2017), p. 119.

79. IMF (International Monetary Fund), *World Economic Outlook: Gaining Momentum?* (Washington, DC: IMF, 2017).

80. James Manyika and others, *A New Look at the Declining Labor Share of Income in the United States* (San Francisco: McKinsey Global Institute, 2019).

81. Mai Chi Dao, Mitali Das, Zsoka Koczan and Weicheng Lian, 'Drivers of declining labour shares of income', IMF blog (12 April 2017), www.imf.org/en/Blogs/Articles/2017/04/12/drivers-of-declining-labor-share-of-income; Mai Chi Dao, Mitali Das, Zsoka Koczan and Weicheng Lian, *Why is Labor Receiving a Smaller Share of Global Income? Theory and Empirical Evidence*, IMF Working Paper no. 17/169 (Washington, DC, July 2017).

82. UNCTAD, *Beyond Austerity: Towards a Global New Deal*, p. 138.

83. Luigi Zingales, *Towards a Political Theory of the Firm*. New Working Paper Series no. 10, Stigler Center for the Study of the Economy and the State (Chicago: University of Chicago, 2017).

84. Michael Ignatieff, *The Rights Revolution* (Toronto: House of Anansi Press, 2000), p. 92.

85. Joachim H. Spangenberg, 'Institutional change for strong sustainable consumption: Sustainable consumption and the degrowth economy', *Sustainability: Science, Practice and Policy* 10(1) (2014), pp. 62–77.

3 The Strange Persistence of the Ideology of Growth

1. World Bank, 'Jobs and development' (April 2023), www.world bank.org/en/topic/jobsanddevelopment/overview

2. ILO, *World Employment and Social Outlook: Trends 2022* (Geneva: International Labour Office, 2022), p. 44.

3. Ibid., p. 45.

4. World Bank, *World Development Report 2019: The Changing Nature of Work* (Washington, DC: World Bank, 2019), pp. 20 and 24.

5. Sangheon Lee et al., *Does Economic Growth Deliver Jobs? Revisiting Okun's Law*, ILO Working Paper 17 (Geneva: November 2020).

6. OECD (2023), General government debt (indicator). doi: 10.1787/a0528cc2-en (accessed 22 July 2023).

7. Laura Feiveson and John Sabelhaus, *How Does Intergenerational Wealth Transmission Affect Wealth Concentration?* (Washington, DC: Board of Governors of the Federal Reserve System, 1 June 2018).

8. Facundo Alvaredo, Bertrand Garbinti and Thomas Piketty, 'On the share of inheritance in aggregate wealth: Europe and the USA, 1900–2010', *Economica* 84 (2017), pp. 239–60.

9. Households in the top 1 per cent receive as much as 18 per cent of the total amount transferred in Germany and the United States, while the share going to the bottom 25 per cent is very low. See Brian Nolan, Juan C. Palomino, Philippe van Kerm and Salvatore Morelli, *The Wealth of Families: The Intergenerational Transmission of Wealth in Britain in Comparative Perspective* (London: Nuffield Foundation, August 2020). Across OECD countries, inheritances and gifts explain 72 per cent of the wealth of the 20 per cent richest households, and less than 1.5 per cent of the (much less significant) wealth of the bottom 20 per cent; and the wealthiest 20 per

cent households report 50 times more such transfers; OECD, *A Broken Social Elevator? How to Promote Social Mobility* (Paris: OECD, 2018), p. 206.

10. There are important differences between countries, of course: in the United States, only 0.2 per cent of estates are subject to inheritance taxes, and parents may transfer up to $11 million to their children exempt of taxes, while the figures are 48 per cent and $17,000 for the Region of Brussels-Capital in Belgium. See OECD, *Inheritance Taxation in OECD Countries* (Paris: OECD, 2021).

11. David Kenert and Cameron Hepburn, 'Making carbon pricing work for citizens', CEPR Policy Portal (31 July 2018), https://voxeu.org/article/making-carbon-pricing-work-citizens

12. H. Scharin and J. Wallström, *The Swedish CO_2 Tax – An Overview* (Stockholm: Anthesis Enveco AB, 2018), p. 23. This, however, only accounts for territorial emissions, in other words, it does not include emissions embedded in imports into Sweden. Moreover, the reduction in emissions from fossil energies can also be explained by the fact that Sweden can count on hydro power and biomass from the forest as renewable sources of energy.

13. Christophe De Gouvello, Dominique Finon and Pierre Guigon, *Reconciling Carbon Pricing and Energy Policies in Developing Countries: Integrating Policies for a Clean Energy Transition* (Washington, DC: World Bank, 2020), pp. 121 and 189.

14. World Bank Group, *State and Trends of Carbon Pricing 2019* (Washington, DC: World Bank, p. 81).

15. Brian Murray and Nicholas Rivers, 'British Columbia's revenue-neutral carbon tax: A review of the latest "grand experiment" in environmental policy', *Energy Policy* 86 (2015), pp. 674–83.

16. World Bank Group, *State and Trends of Carbon Pricing 2019* (Washington, DC: World Bank, 2019), p. 81.

17. Darragh Conway, Johannes Ackva, Axel Michaelowa, Barbara Hermann, Constanze Haug, Aglaja Espelage et al., *Tipping the Balance: Lessons on Building Support for Carbon Prices*. Policy Brief commissioned by the Deutsche Gesellschaft für Internationale Zusammenarbeit (GIZ) GmbH on behalf of the German Federal Ministry for the Environment, Nature Conservation and Nuclear

Safety (BMU) (Berlin/Amsterdam/Freiburg: Adelphi/Climate Focus/Perspectives Climate Group, 2019).

18. David Klenert, Linus Mattauch, Emmanuel Combet, Ottmar Edenhofer, Cameron Hepburn, Ryan Rafaty et al., 'Making carbon pricing work for citizens', *Nature Climate Change* 8(8) (2018), pp. 667–77.

19. For a systematic discussion, see *Non-take-up of Rights in the Context of Social Protection*, Report of the Special Rapporteur on extreme poverty and human rights, Olivier De Schutter, to the fiftieth session of the Human Rights Council (A/HRC/50/38, April 2022).

20. Herman E. Daly, *Beyond Growth: The Economics of Sustainable Development* (New York: Beacon Press, 1976).

21. Herman E. Daly, *Steady-state Economics* (Washington, DC: Island Press, 1977); Claus Offe, 'The Utopia of the zero-option: Modernity and modernization as normative political criteria', *Praxis International* 7(1) (1987), pp. 1–24.

22. Heloise Weber and Martin Weber, 'When means of implementation meet Ecological Modernization Theory: A critical frame for thinking about the Sustainable Development Goals initiative', *World Development* 136 (2020), 105129.

4   The Post-growth Approach to Combating Poverty

1. ILO, *World Employment and Social Outlook: Trends 2022* (Geneva: ILO, 2022), p. 45.

2. Paul Collier and Anke Hoeffler, *On Economic Causes of Civil War*, Oxford Economic Papers 50 (1998), pp. 563–73; Jeffrey D. Sachs and Andrew M. Warner, *Natural Resource Abundance and Economic Growth*, National Bureau of Economic Research Working Paper no. w5398; original 1995, revised 1999, www.nber.org/papers/w5398; Frederick Van der Ploeg, *Challenges and Opportunities for Resource Rich Economies*, CEPR Discussion Paper no. 5688 (2006); Marcatan Humphreys et al. (eds) *Escaping the Resource Curse* (New York: Columbia University Press, 2007).

3. Daly, *Steady-state Economics*.

4. I am indebted to Adrian Smith, my esteemed colleague from the University of Sussex Business School, for having generously shared his views on this issue with me.

5. The notion of 'social carrier of techniques' was initially proposed in a paper by Charles Edquist and Olle Edquist, 'Social carriers of techniques for development', *Journal of Peace Research*, 16(4) (1979): 313–31. Their conclusion is that whereas the wider use of labour-intensive techniques in developing countries would serve to combat unemployment, such techniques will not in fact be prioritized, since: 'the problem is not primarily technical: it is first and foremost political, social and economic. For the possible and available labour-intensive techniques to be used, obstacles in the form of vested interests and power structures must be overcome. New actual social carriers must emerge to introduce or generate these new techniques – and these new carriers will inevitably be in conflict with established power groups, as they necessarily will represent a challenge to entrenched interests.'

6. Ernst F. Schumacher, *Small Is Beautiful* (New York: Harper & Row, 1973); Jacques Ellul, *The Technological Society* (New York: Vintage, 1964).

7. See Philippe Bihouix, *L'âge des low tech* (Paris: Seuil, 2014). The notion of 'conviviality' has its source in the work of Ivan Illich, *Tools for Conviviality* (New York: Harper & Row, 1973).

8. Adrian Smith and Mariano Fressoli, 'Post-automation', *Futures* 132 (2021), 102778.

9. Mario Pansera and Mariano Fressoli, 'Innovation without growth: Frameworks for understanding technological change in a post-growth era', *Organization* 28(3) (2021), pp. 380–404.

10. On the importance of social innovations and the role of local communities in designing solutions to the challenges they face, see in particular Kerry McCarthy, *The Ecology of Innovation* (Peterborough: Citizen Power Peterborough, 2010); Adrian Smith, Mariano Fressoli, Dinesh Abrol, Elisa Around and Adrian Ely, *Grassroots Innovation Movements* (London: Routledge, 2016); and Olivier De Schutter and Tom Dedeurwaerdere, *Social Innovation in the Service of Social and Ecological Transformation: The Rise of the Enabling State* (London: Routledge, 2022); as well as

Frank Moulaert (ed.), *International Handbook on Social Innovation: Collective Action, Social Learning and Transdisciplinary Research* (Cheltenham: Edward Elgar, 2010).

11. The measures listed below are detailed and expanded on in the report I submitted to the UN General Assembly at its 75th session. See *The 'Just Transition' in the Economic Recovery: Eradicating Poverty within Planetary Boundaries*. Report of the Special Rapporteur on extreme poverty and human rights to the 75th session of the General Assembly (A/75/181/Rev.1) (2020).

12. Each $1 million spent on energy efficiency supports 7.72 jobs, while similar expenditures in the renewable and fossil fuel sectors create 7.49 and 2.65 jobs, respectively. See Heidi Garrett-Peltier, 'Green versus brown: Comparing the employment impacts of energy efficiency, renewable energy, and fossil fuels using an input-output model', *Economic Modelling* 61 (2017), pp. 439–47.

13. UN Department of Economic and Social Affairs, *Accelerating SDG7 Achievement: Policy Briefs in support of the first SDG7 review at the UN High-Level Political Forum 2018* (New York, 2018), p. 104.

14. Solar photovoltaic electricity, for example, requires 0.87 total person years for each GWh of electricity generated while electricity from coal or natural gas requires 0.11. See Max Wei, Shana Patadia and Daniel Kammen, 'Putting renewables and energy efficiency to work: How many jobs can the clean energy industry generate in the U.S.?', *Energy Policy* 38(2) (2010), pp. 919–31.

15. Ying Chen, *Renewable Energy Investment and Employment in China*, Political Economy Research Institute (PERI) Working Paper Series 439 (Amherst: University of Massachusetts, 2017).

16. ILO and UN Environment Programme, *Working Towards Sustainable Development: Opportunities for Decent Work and Social Inclusion in a Green Economy* (Geneva: ILO, 2012), p. 75.

17. International Renewable Energy Agency, *Renewable Energy and Jobs – Annual Review 2016* (Abu Dhabi, UAE: IRENA, 2016), p. 13.

18. UN Department of Economic and Social Affairs, *Accelerating SDG7 Achievement: Policy Briefs in Support of the First SDG Review* (New York, 2019), pp. 104–9.

19. International Energy Agency (IEA), International Renewable Energy Agency (IRENA), the UN Statistics Division, World Bank and World Health Organization (WHO), *Tracking SDG 7: The Energy Progress Report 2019* (New York: United Nations, 2019), p. 75.

20. Christian Dupraz et al., 'Combining solar photovoltaic panels and food crops for optimising land use: Towards new agrivoltaic schemes', *Renewable Energy* 36(10), pp. 2725–32.

21. UN Research Institute for Social Development, *Policy Innovations for Transformative Change* (Geneva: UNRISD, 2016), p. 152.

22. The access rate in rural areas was 79 per cent in 2017, much lower than the urban access rate of 97 per cent. UN Department of Economic and Social Affairs, *Accelerating SDG7 Achievement*, p. 16.

23. See https://sdgs.un.org/goals/goal7

24. UN Department of Economic and Social Affairs, *Accelerating SDG7 Achievement*, p. 79.

25. Anna Maria Oosthuizen, Roula Inglesi-Lotz and George Alex Thopil, 'The relationship between renewable energy and retail electricity prices: Panel evidence from OECD countries', *Energy* 238-B (2022), 121790. https://doi.org/10.1016/j.energy.2021.121790.

26. International Renewable Energy Agency, *Renewable Power Generation Costs in 2017* (Abu Dhabi, UAE, 2018), p. 4; Cristina Ballester and Dolores Furió, 'Effects of renewables on the stylized facts of electricity prices', *Renewable and Sustainable Energy Reviews* 52 (2015), pp. 1596–609.

27. See https://unstats.un.org/sdgs/report/2019/Goal-11/

28. UN Environmental Programme, *Buildings and Climate Change: Summary for Decision Makers* (Nairobi: UNEP, 2009).

29. UN Environmental Programme, 'Join the global platform for sustainable buildings', *UNEP Sustainable Buildings and Climate Initiative: Promoting Policies and Practices for Sustainability* (Nairobi, 2017).

30. UN Environmental Programme, *Buildings and Climate Change: Summary for Decision Makers*, p. 9.

31. ILO, *Green Jobs in Construction: Small Changes – Big Effect* (Geneva: ILO, 2010).

32. UN Habitat, *Sustainable Housing for Sustainable Cities: A Policy Framework for Developing Countries* (Nairobi, 2012).

33. Ibid.; and Ramin Keivani, Joseph H.M. Tah, Esra Kurul and Henry Abanda, *Green Jobs Creation through Sustainable Refurbishment in Developing Countries*, ILO Working Paper 275 (Geneva, 2005) (providing examples from Brazil, South Africa and The Netherlands).

34. ILO, *World Employment and Social Outlook 2018: Greening with Jobs* (Geneva: ILO, 2018), p. 42.

35. Ibid., p. 24.

36. See Norman E. Borlaug and Christopher Dowswell, *The Green Revolution: An Unfinished Agenda*, CFS Distinguished Lecture Series Thirtieth Session (Rome: Committee on World Food Security, 23–24 September 2004); Norman E. Borlaug, 1970 Nobel Peace Prize Laureate, Special 30th Anniversary Lecture at the Norwegian Nobel Institute: 'The Green Revolution revisited and the road ahead' (8 September 2000).

37. According to the United States Census Bureau, the annual population growth rate peaked at 2.19 per cent in 1963, decreasing to 1.14 per cent by 2013. *International Programs: World Population Growth Rates: 1950–2050*, U.S. Census Bureau (see www.census.gov). The UN Population Division of the UN Department on Economic and Social Affairs estimates that the peak in the rate of demographic growth was reached in 1965–70, at an annual rate of 2.04 per cent; the rate of growth was 1.31 per cent in 1999–2000. See UN Department of Economic and Social Affairs Population Division, *The World at Six Billion*, ch. 10, Fig. 2, UN Doc. ESA/P/WP.154 (1999).

38. Paul R. Ehrlich, *The Population Bomb* (San Francisco: Sierra Club/Ballantine Books, 1968).

39. Plenary of the IPBES, 'Summary for policymakers of the global assessment of biodiversity and ecosystem services', 7th session held in Paris in May 2019 (Bonn: IPBES Secretariat, 2019), https://doi.org/10.5281/zenodo.3553579.

40. Ibid.

41. Pete Smith et al., 'Agriculture', in Bert Metz et al. (eds), *Climate Change 2007: Mitigation*. Contribution of Working Group III to

the Fourth Assessment Report of the Inter-governmental Panel on Climate Change (New York: Cambridge University Press, 2007), pp. 498–550.

42. Tara Garnett, 'Food sustainability: Problems, perspectives and solutions', *Proceedings of the Nutrition Society* 72 (2013), pp. 29–39.

43. Attempts are made to assess the 'true costs' of food production, in projects such as TEEBAgriFood (housed at UNEP and led by the Economics of the Ecosystems and Biodiversity [TEEB Office).

44. Barry Popkin, Camila Corvalan and Laurance M. Grummer-Strawn, 'Dynamics of the double burden of malnutrition and the changing nutrition reality', *The Lancet* 395(10217) (January 2020), pp. 65–74; Adam Drewnowski, 'The economics of food choice behavior: Why poverty and obesity are linked', in Adam Drewnowski and Barbara Rolls (eds), *Obesity Treatment and Prevention: New Directions* (Basil: Nestec Ltd, Vevey/S Karger AG, 2012), pp. 95–112. The rise of obesity is no longer limited to high-income countries, but has become a major concern in most countries of Latin America and the Caribbean, eastern Europe and Central and East Asia (China and Indonesia). The sociological patterns differ from region to region, however; whereas obesity primarily affects low-income households in rich countries, by contrast, obesity increases are largest among wealthier households in countries in sub-Saharan Africa and South Asia which are still undergoing a nutrition transition. See also Boyd Swinburn et al., 'The global syndemic of obesity, undernutrition, and climate change: The Lancet Commission report', *The Lancet* 393(10173), pp. 791–846.

45. Franco Sassi, *L'obésité et l'économie de la prévention: objectif santé* (Paris: OECD, 2010), pp. 83–4.

46. *Agroecology and the Right to Food*, Report submitted by the Special Rapporteur on the right to food, Olivier De Schutter, to the 16th session of the Human Rights Council (A/HRC/16/49) (2010).

47. Robert Scholes et al., *Summary for Policymakers of the Assessment Report on Land Degradation and Restoration of the Intergovernmental Science-Policy Platform on Biodiversity and Ecosystem Services* (Bonn: IPBES, 2018).

48. Priyadarshi Shukla et al., 'Summary for policymakers', in *Climate Change and Land: An IPCC Special Report on Climate Change, Desertification, Land Degradation, Sustainable Land Management, Food Security, and Greenhouse Gas Fluxes in Terrestrial Ecosystems* (Intergovernmental Panel of Experts on Climate Change, 2019), https://www.ipcc.ch/srccl/chapter/summary-for-policy makers/ (accessed 4 December 2023).

49. Global Sustainable Development Report, *The Future is Now – Science for Achieving Sustainable Development* (2019), https://sustainabledevelopment.un.org/content/documents/24797GSDR_report_2019.pdf (accessed 4 December 2023).

50. Global Center on Adaptation and World Resources Institute, *Adapt Now: A Global Call for Leadership on Climate Resilience* (The Netherlands and Washington, DC, 2019).

51. IPES-Food, *From Uniformity to Diversity: A Paradigm Shift from Industrial Agriculture to Diversified Agroecological Systems* (Brussels, 2016); Food and Agriculture Organization, *Scaling Up Agroecology Initiative: Transforming Food and Agricultural Systems in Support of the SDGs* (Rome, 2018).

52. High-Level Panel of Experts of the Committee on World Food Security (HLPE), *Agroecological and Other Innovative Approaches for Sustainable Agriculture and Food Systems that Enhance Food Security and Nutrition* (Rome: FAO, 2019).

53. UN Economic Commission for Europe, *From Transition to Transformation: Sustainable and Inclusive Development in Europe and Central Asia* (Geneva, 2012).

54. OECD, *ITF Transport Outlook 2019* (Paris: OECD, 2019).

55. The International Energy Agency (IEA) provides regular updates on the contribution of the energy sector to CO_2 emissions. See: www.iea.org/topics/global-energy-transitions-stocktake

56. UN Economic Commission for Europe, *From Transition to Transformation*.

57. Gordon Mitchell and Danny Dorling, 'An environmental justice analysis of British air quality', *Environment and Planning A* 35(5) (2003), pp. 909–29.

58. Noel Smith et al., 'Accessibility and capability: The minimum transport needs and costs of rural households', *Journal of Transport Geography* 21 (2012), pp. 93–101.

59. OECD, *ITF Transport Outlook 2019* (2019), https://read.oecd-ilibrary.org/transport/itf-transport-outlook-2019_transp_outlook-en-2019-en#page1 (accessed 4 December 2023).

60. Heidi Enzler, 'Air travel for private purposes: An analysis of airport access, income and environmental concern in Switzerland', *Journal of Transport Geography* 61 (2017), pp. 1–8.

61. Helena Titheridge, Nicola Christie, Roger Mackett, Daniel Oviedo Hernández and Runing Ye, *Transport and Poverty: A Review of the Evidence* (University College London, 2014).

62. UK Government, Department for Business, Energy & Industrial Strategy, *UK Government GHG Conversion Factors for Company Reporting* (London, 2019).

63. Tim Cresswell, Jane Yeonjae Lee, Anna Nikolaeva, André Nóvoa and Cristina Temenos, *Moving Towards Transition: Commoning Mobility for a Low-carbon Future* (London: Bloomsbury, 2022).

64. Mark Nieuwenhuijsen and Haneen Khreis, 'Car-free cities: Pathway to healthy urban living', *Environment International* 94 (2016), pp. 251–62.

65. Qiyang Liu, Karen Lucas, Greg Marsden and Yang Liu, 'Egalitarianism and public perception of social inequities: A case study of Beijing congestion charge', *Transport Policy* 74 (2019), pp. 47–62.

66. International Energy Agency, *Global EV Outlook 2019* (Paris, 2019).

67. Rachana Vidhi and Prassana Shrivastava, 'A review of electric vehicle lifecycle emissions and policy recommendations to increase EV penetration in India', *Energies* 11(3) (2018), p. 483. The use of rechargeable lithium-ion batteries to power electric vehicles and energy storage units requires the mining of battery metals, which has led to the contamination of water bodies and other forms of pollution, dam disasters, and the forced eviction of communities. Strict regulation of the mining industry should be introduced to avoid such harms in the future.

68. Jason Henderson, 'EVs are not the answer: A mobility justice critique of electric vehicle transitions', *Annals of the American Association of Geographers* 110 (2020), pp. 1993–2010.

69. ILO, *Jobs in Green and Healthy Transport: Making the Green Shift* (Geneva: ILO, 2019) p. 30.

70. Gary Becker, *Human Capital: A Theoretical and Empirical Analysis, with Special Reference to Education* (Chicago: University of Chicago Press, 1962).

71. See Miles Corak, 'Income inequality, equality of opportunity, and intergenerational mobility', *Journal of Economic Perspectives* 27(3) (2013), pp. 79–102; or Thomas Bossuroy and Denis Cogneau, 'Social mobility in five African countries', *Review of Income and Wealth* 59(S1) (2013), pp. 84–110. For a more systematic analysis, see *The Persistence of Poverty: How Real Equality Can Break the Vicious Cycles*, Report of the Special Rapporteur on extreme poverty and human rights, Olivier De Schutter, to the 76th session of the General Assembly (A/76/177) (2021); and Olivier De Schutter, Hugh Frazer, Anne-Catherine Guio and Eric Marlier, *The Escape from Poverty: Breaking the Vicious Cycles Perpetuating Disadvantage* (Bristol: Policy Press, 2023), pp. 14–15.

72. A comprehensive review of the links between equality and sustainability has been provided elsewhere. Inequality not only makes people more materialistic and stimulates unsustainable modes of consumption, it also inhibits civic and political participation, which is essential to ensuring that large-scale transformations are sufficiently legitimate and supported across all society. Conversely, more equal societies encourage pro-social and pro-environmental behaviour: people in more equal societies express a greater concern for others and for the common good, which makes it easier for them to contribute to the achievement of certain collectively defined objectives. For developments, see Olivier De Schutter and Tom Dedeurwaerdere, *Social Innovation in the Service of Ecological and Social Transformation: The Rise of the Enabling State* (London: Routledge, 2021), ch. 5.

73. Thorstein Veblen, *Theory of the Leisure Class* (New York: Macmillan, 1899), p. 64.

74. Ibid.

75. See, for a systematic review of the evidence, Olivier De Schutter, Kate Pickett and Richard Wilkinson, 'Equality as an ingredient for a post-growth world', in K. Arabadjieva, N. Countouris, B. Luna Fabris and W. Zwysen (eds), *Transformative Ideas – Ensuring a Just Share of Progress for All* (Brussels: European Trade Union Institute, 2023), pp. 81–92.

76. Richard Wilkinson and Kate Pickett, *The Spirit Level: Why Greater Equality Makes Societies Stronger* (London: Allen Lane, 2009), p. 226.

77. Global Chance, 'Des questions qui fâchent: contribution au débat national sur la transition énergétique', *Les Cahiers de Global Chance* 33 (2013).

78. Fabrice Lenglart, Christophe Lesieur and Jean-Louis Pasquier, *Les émissions de CO$_2$ du circuit économique en France* (Paris: Insee Références, 2010).

79. Siddharth Prakash et al., *Influence of the Service Life of Products in Terms of their Environmental Impact: Establishing an Information Base and Developing Strategies against 'Obsolescence'* (Bonn: Umweltbundesamt, 2020); Eric Vidalenc and Laurent Meunier, *Another Perspective on Environmental Impacts of Planned Obsolescence* (Paris: European Council for an Energy Efficient Economy, 2015).

80. Yatish Joshi and Zillur Rahman, 'Factors affecting green purchase behavior and future research directions', *International Strategic Management Review* 3(1–2) (2015), pp. 128–43.

81. Cornelis Peter Balde et al., *The Global E-waste Monitor: Quantities, Flows, and Resources* (Bonn, Geneva, Vienna: UN University, International Communication Union & International Solid Waste Association, 2018).

82. Michelle Heackock et al., 'E-waste and harm to vulnerable populations: A growing global problem', *Environmental Health Perspectives* 124(5) (2016), pp. 550–5.

83. Karin Lundgren, *The Global Impact of E-waste: Addressing the Challenge* (Geneva: ILO Programme on Safety and Health at Work and the Environment, 2012).

84. Michelle Heackock et al., 'E-waste and harm to vulnerable populations: A growing global problem', *Environmental Health Perspectives* 124(5) (2016), pp. 550–5.

85. European Economic and Social Committee. Opinion (2014/C 67/05) on 'Towards more sustainable consumption: Industrial product lifetimes and restoring trust through consumer information', *Official Journal C* 67, 6 March 2014, p. 23.

86. ILO, *World Employment and Social Outlook 2018: Greening with Jobs* (Geneva: ILO, 2018), p. 52.

87. Scitovsky, *The Joyless Economy*, p. 8.

88. Jordi Teixidó-Figueras, Julia K. Steinberger, Fridolin Krausmann, Helmut Haberl, Thomas Wiedmann, Glen P. Peters et al., 'International inequality of environmental pressures: Decomposition and comparative analysis', *Ecological Indicators* 62 (2016), pp. 163–73.

89. In 2019, 21 per cent of workers lived in poverty (living on less than US$3.10 per day), including 8 per cent who were in extreme poverty (living on less than US$1.90 per day): for approximately 712 million people therefore, a job did not guarantee a decent life for themselves and their families. See Rosina Gammarano, 'The working poor ... or how job is no guarantee of decent living conditions', ILOSTAT Spotlight on Work Statistics, No. 6 (Geneva: ILO, 2019), p. 5.

90. The European Union defines the working poor as people who are employed (have a job for at least seven months during the reference year) but whose incomes are below 60 per cent of the national median equivalized disposable income (representing the amount of money that an individual or household earns after taxes and other deductions have been taken out, adjusted for the size and composition of the household). The data are from 2017: Eurofound, *In-work Poverty in the EU* (Dublin, 2017), p. 5.

91. Nicole Aubert and Vincent de Gaulejac, *Le coût de l'excellence* (Paris: Seuil, rééd. 2007); Christophe Dejours, *Souffrance en France: la banalisation de l'injustice sociale* (Paris: Seuil, 1998); Vincent de Gaulejac, *Travail, les raisons de la colère* (Paris: Seuil, 2015).

92. See Mark Granovetter, *Getting a Job* (Chicago: University of Chicago Press, 2nd edn 1995); Linda Datcher Loury, 'Some contacts are fairer than others: Informal networks, job tenures, and wages', *Journal of Labor Economics* 24(2) (2006), pp. 299–318.

93. Jonathan Mijs, 'The paradox of inequality: Income inequality and belief in meritocracy go hand in hand', *Socio-Economic Review* 19(1) (2019), pp. 7–35; Nicholas Heiserman and Brent Simpson, 'Higher inequality increases the gap in the perceived merit of the rich and poor', *Social Psychology Quarterly* 80(3) (2017), pp. 243–53.

94. Karlijin L.A. Roex, Tim Huijts, and Inge Sieben, 'Attitudes towards income inequality: "Winners" versus "losers" of the perceived meritocracy', *Acta Sociologica*, 62(1) (2019), pp. 47–63.

95. Robert Walker, *The Shame of Poverty* (Oxford: Oxford University Press, 2014), pp. 132–56.

96. Hannah B. Waldfogel, Jennifer Sheehy-Skeffington, Oliver P. Hauser and Nour S. Kteily, 'Ideology selectively shapes attention to inequality', *Proceedings of the National Academy of Sciences* 118(14) (2021).

97. Michael Sandel, *Tyranny of Merit: What's Become of the Common Good?* (New York: Farrar, Straus and Giroux, 2021).

98. Martin J. Watts and William F. Mitchell, 'The costs of unemployment in Australia', *Economic and Labour Relations Review* 11(2) (2000), pp. 180–97. At the individual level, the consequences of unemployment go beyond a lack of income: see Amartya K. Sen, 'Inequality, unemployment and contemporary Europe', *International Labour Review* 136(2) (1997), pp. 155–71.

99. OECD, 'Public unemployment spending' (indicator). Available at https://doi.org/10.1787/55557fd4-en. In part, the relatively modest proportion of the GDP that goes to compensating the loss of income from unemployment can be explained by the fact that not all adults who do not work are effectively compensated. Some job-seekers receive no compensation: even in high-income countries, only 52.2 per cent of unemployed people received cash benefits, either because they are not eligible, or because their right to unemployment benefits has expired, or because they don't manage to overcome the administrative hurdles, leading

to non-take-up. See, for the numbers, ILO, *World Social Protection Report 2020–22* (Geneva: ILO), p. 158, Figure 4.29; and, on non-take-up, *The Non-take-up of Rights in the Context of Social Protection*, Report of the Special Rapporteur on extreme poverty and human rights, Olivier De Schutter, to the 50th session of the Human Rights Council (A/HRC/50/38, 1 April 2022). And some individuals without employment do not register as job-seekers because they are discouraged or because they cannot reconcile work with household responsibilities, such as providing care to children or to dependent older persons: in the European Union and in the United States, only around half of those seeking employment are officially unemployed. See Pavlina Tcherneva and Aurore Lalucq, *A Job Guarantee for Europe* (Brussels: Foundation for European Progressive Studies, September 2022); Pavlina Tcherneva, 'The federal job guarantee: Prevention, not just a cure', *Challenge* 62(4) (2019), p. 5.

100. Tcherneva, 'The federal job guarantee: Prevention, not just a cure'.

101. Steven Raphael and Rudolf Winter-Ebmer, 'Identifying the effect of unemployment on crime', *Journal of Law and Economics* 44(1) (2001), pp. 259–83 (noting the positive relationship that exists in the context of the United States between unemployment rates and property crimes, as well as, to a limited extent, the violent crime of rape).

102. Eva Van Belle, Valentina Di Stasio, Ralf Caers, Marijke De Couck and Stijn Baert, 'Why are employers put off by long spells of unemployment?', *European Sociological Review* 34(6) (2018), pp. 694–710.

103. Felix Oberholzer-Gee, 'Nonemployment stigma as rational herding: A field experiment', *Journal of Economic Behavior & Organization* 65(1) (2008), pp. 30–40.

104. Karsten Paul and Klaus Moser, 'Unemployment impairs mental health: Meta-analyses', *Journal of Vocational Behavior* 74 (2009), pp. 264–82. It has been shown that rates of suicide and other causes of death related to a loss of employment and income increased, especially among white males, in the US counties where industrial activity would be most affected by the entry of China into

the World Trade Organization (or, more precisely, by the granting to China of 'Permanent Normal Trade Relations' [PNTR] status), due to the feared impacts on employment in blue-collar jobs: Justin R. Pierce and Peter K. Schott, 'Trade liberalization and mortality: Evidence from US counties', *American Economic Review: Insights* 2(1) (2020), pp. 47–64.

105. Daniel Sullivan and Till Von Wachter, 'Job displacement and mortality: An analysis using administrative data', *Quarterly Journal of Economics* 124(3) (2009), pp. 1265–306, p. 1266.

106. T.A. Blakely, S. Collings and J. Atkinson, 'Unemployment and suicide: Evidence for a causal association?', *Journal of Epidemiology and Community Health* 57 (2003), pp. 594–600, p. 596.

107. William F. Mitchell, 'The buffer stock employment model – full employment without a NAIRU', *Journal of Economic Issues* 32(2) (1998), pp. 547–55; Pavlina R. Tcherneva, *The Case for a Job Guarantee* (Cambridge: Polity, 2020).

108. Melvin Brodsky, 'Public-service employment programs in selected OECD countries', *Monthly Labor Review* (October 2000).

109. Nicolas Bueno, 'From productive work to capability-enhancing work: Implications for labour law and policy', *Journal of Human Development and Capabilities* 23(3) (2022), pp. 354–72. See also Andrea Veltman, *Meaningful Work* (Oxford: Oxford University Press, 2016).

110. See https://democratizingwork.org/

111. In the United States, the Treaty of Detroit, negotiated in 1950 between General Motors (at the time the largest manufacturing company in the country) and the Union of Automobile Workers (UAW), came to symbolize this compromise. See Leo Panitch and Sam Gindin, *The Making of Global Capitalism: The Political Economy of American Empire* (London: Verso, 2012), pp. 83–4.

112. Timothy Weidel, 'Moving towards a capability for meaningful labour', *Journal of Human Development and Capabilities* 19(1) (2018), pp. 70–88. The 'capability for meaningful work' here refers to 'being able to freely and successfully pursue an avenue by which a person can engage in meaningful labour, interacting with some aspect of nature (as well as other human beings) in a way that develops their faculties, utilizes practical reasoning, and

provides them with a sense of dignity'. See also Lucas McGranahan, 'Meaningful labour, employee ownership, and workplace democracy: A comment on Weidel (2018)', *Journal of Human Development and Capabilities* 21(4) (2020), pp. 389–97 (noting how employee-owned businesses and cooperatives contribute to such capability).

113. Michael Jacobs and Mariana Mazzucato (eds), *Rethinking Capitalism: Economics and Policy for Sustainable and Inclusive Growth* (Chichester: John Wiley & Sons, 2016).

114. Isabelle Ferreras, *Firms as Political Entities: Saving Democracy through Economic Bicameralism* (Cambridge: Cambridge University Press, 2017).

115. ILO, *Global Wage Report 2016/2017: Wage Inequality in the Workplace* (Geneva: ILO, 2017).

116. Daron Acemoglu and Pascual Restrepo, *Robots and Jobs: Evidence from US Labor Markets*, Working Paper 23285 (Washington, DC: NBER, 2017); David Autor, 'Why are there still so many jobs? The history and future of workplace automation', *Journal of Economic Perspectives* 29 (2015), pp. 3–30.

117. Whether total working time will necessarily fall in a low-carbon society remains debatable, however, since the reduction in economic output would be compensated for at least in part by the switch to more labour-intensive types of activity, such as low-input farming or renewable energy (the production of which, as seen above, will result in creating more jobs than will be lost in the fossil fuel sectors). More generally, the introduction of 'triple-dividend' measures (including the examples provided above) aims to ensure that the ecological transformation of societies will spread employment opportunities more widely.

118. For more detailed studies on the impacts of working time reduction, see Anna Coote, Jane Franklin, Andrew Simms and Mary Murphy, *21 Hours: Why a Shorter Working Week Can Help Us All to Flourish in the 21st Century* (London: New Economics Foundation, 2010); Dominique Méda and Pierre Larrouturou, *Einstein avait raison: il faut réduire le temps de travail* (Ivry-sur-Seine: Editions de l'Atelier, 2016); Stan De Spiegelaere and Agnieszka

Piasna, *The Why and How of Working Time Reduction* (Brussels: ETUI, 2017).

119. De Spiegelaere and Piasna, *The Why and How of Working Time Reduction*, pp. 27–8.

120. Ruth Simpson, 'Presenteeism, power and organizational change: Long hours as a career barrier and the impact on the working lives of women managers', *British Journal of Management* 9 (1998), pp. 37–50; Sarah Rutherford, 'Are you going home already?', *Time & Society* 10(2–3) (2001), pp. 259–76.

121. On the decline of social capital in the period 1975–2000 in the context of the United States, see Putnam, *Bowling Alone*.

122. Benjamin Kline Hunnicutt, *Kellogg's Six-hour Day* (Philadelphia, PA: Temple University Press, 1996).

123. Juliet B. Schor, *The Overworked American: The Unexpected Decline of Leisure* (New York: Basic Books, 1992); Juliet B. Schor, 'Global inequality and environmental crisis: An argument for reducing working hours in the North', *World Development* 19(1) (1991), pp. 73–84.

124. Indeed, it may be recalled that in 1974 it was in order to reduce energy consumption in the face of high energy prices resulting from a miners' strike that the British government, then under the Conservative leadership of Prime Minister Edward Heath, decided that commercial electricity users (with the exception of essential services) could only function for a maximum of three days per week, with no possibilities for overtime work. The 'experiment' lasted for two months. After Labour won the elections, an agreement was reached with the National Union of Mineworkers and the three-day week ended on 8 March 1974. During the period of the experiment, economic output dropped only slightly, by 6 per cent, since reduced working hours were compensated for by increased productivity and lower absenteeism rates. But the social impacts were significant, with about 1.5 million additional workers registering as unemployed.

125. Specifically, the study concluded that a 10 per cent reduction in work hours would result in the decline of the ecological footprint, carbon footprint and CO_2 emissions of 12.1 per cent, 14.6 per cent, and 4.2 per cent, respectively. See Kyle W. Knight, Eugene

A. Rosa and Juliet B. Schor, 'Reducing growth to achieve environmental sustainability: The role of work hours', in Jeannette Wicks-Lim and Robert Pollin (eds), *Capitalism on Trial: Explorations in the Tradition of Thomas E. Weisskopf* (Cheltenham: Edward Elgar, 2013), pp. 187–204.

126. Jonas Nässén and Jörgen Larsson, 'Would shorter working time reduce greenhouse gas emissions? An analysis of time use and consumption in Swedish households', *Environment and Planning C: Government and Policy* 33(4) (2015), pp. 726–45.

127. Jared B. Fitzgerald, Juliet B. Schor and Andrew K. Jorgenson. 'Working hours and carbon dioxide emissions in the United States, 2007–2013', *Social Forces* 96(4) (2018), pp. 1851–74.

128. Mikko Jalas, 'A time use perspective on the materials intensity of consumption', *Ecological Economics* 41 (2002), pp. 109–23.

129. Some studies conflate both effects in measuring the impact of working hours on the ecological footprint of individuals and households. For instance, a French study finds that households with longer hours of work have higher impact through bigger homes, more transport expenditures and higher expenditures for eating out. See François-Xavier Devetter and Sandrine Rousseau, 'Working hours and sustainable development', *Review of Social Economy* 69(3) (2011), pp. 333–55 (concluding that 'consumption habits are effectively linked to working hours, and not just income.... Some of the most polluting forms of consumption are favoured by long or very long working hours').

130. It is estimated that, in Europe, the reduction of working hours during the period 2007–16 allowed for the creation of an additional 4.5 million jobs. De Spiegelaere and Piasna, *The Why and How of Working Time Reduction*, p. 21.

131. This is what most studies conclude. One study however, comparing working hours and carbon emissions across different states in the United States, finds that the 'composition effect' plays a significant role, as long working hours contribute to carbon-intensive lifestyles due to limited time-affluence. See Jared B. Fitzgerald, Juliet B. Schor and Andrew K. Jorgenson, 'Working hours and carbon dioxide emissions in the United States, 2007–2013', *Social Forces* 96(4) (2018), pp. 1851–74.

132. The shortening of working hours could provide an opportunity to reduce wage gaps within organizations as well, and thus the drive to consumption driven by status-based competition. See Samuel Bowles and Yongjin Park, 'Emulation, inequality, and work hours: Was Thorstein Veblen right?', *Economic Journal* 115 (2005), pp. 397–412.

133. Tim Kasser and Kirk Warren Brown, 'On time, happiness, and ecological footprints', in John De Graaf (ed.), *Take Back Your Time* (San Francisco, CA: Berrett-Koehler Publishers, 2003), pp. 107–12; Tim Kasser and Kennon M. Sheldon, 'Time affluence as a path toward personal happiness and ethical business practice: Empirical evidence from four studies', *Journal of Business Ethics* 84 (2009), pp. 243–55.

134. Steffen Otterbach, 'Mismatches between actual and preferred work time: Empirical evidence of hours constraints in 21 countries', *Journal of Consumer Policy* 33(102) (2010), pp. 143–61.

135. Alberto Alesina, Edward Glaeser and Bruce Sacerdote, 'Work and leisure in the US and Europe: Why so different?', *NBER Macroeconomics Annual 2005* 20 (2005), pp. 1–100.

Conclusion

1. This idea is perhaps nowhere better expressed than in Hickel, *Less Is More*.

Thanks to our Patreon subscriber:

Ciaran Kane

Who has shown generosity and
comradeship in support of our publishing.

Check out the other perks you get by subscribing
to our Patreon – visit patreon.com/plutopress.
Subscriptions start from £3 a month.

The Pluto Press Newsletter

Hello friend of Pluto!

Want to stay on top of the best radical books
we publish?

Then sign up to be the first to hear about our
new books, as well as special events,
podcasts and videos.

You'll also get 50% off your first order with us
when you sign up.

Come and join us!

Go to bit.ly/PlutoNewsletter